LONDON
URBAN
LEGENDS

LONDON
URBAN
LEGENDS

LONDON URBAN LEGENDS

THE CORPSE ON THE TUBE AND OTHER STORIES

SCOTT WOOD

To Clare, Arthur and Alfred Wood: a world of
wondrous stories would mean nothing without you.

First published 2013

The History Press
The Mill, Brimscombe Port
Stroud, Gloucestershire, GL5 2QG
www.thehistorypress.co.uk

© Scott Wood, 2013

The right of Scott Wood to be identified as the Author
of this work has been asserted in accordance with the
Copyright, Designs and Patents Act 1988.

British Library Cataloguing in Publication Data.
A catalogue record for this book is available from the British Library.

ISBN 978 0 7524 8287 3

Typesetting and origination by The History Press
Printed in Great Britain

CONTENTS

ACKNOWLEDGEMENTS

I AM IMMEASURABLY GRATEFUL to my wife Clare anyway, but she not only listened to me as I wittered and wibbled on about this book; she also took the children out so I could write, and fearlessly and methodically undertook the arduous first proofread of this book. I am very, very grateful to you, Clare. Also the greatest of thanks to my family and friends, my colleagues at Bishopsgate Institute and The History Press for their patience, support and trust while I took so damn long writing this book.

Thank you to my friends and those who helped with the book for their advice, guidance, research, encouragement, stories and ears to sound-off into: David V. Barrett, Jason Godwin, Simon Round, Neil Denny, Catherine Halliwell, Sarah Sparkes, Ross McFarlane, Paul Cowdell, Neil Transpontine, Vicky Hill, Caroline Oates, John Rimmer, James Clarke, Matt Brown, Lottie Leedham, Jeremy Harte, Joe McNally, Elizabeth Pinel, Alex Margolis, Mark Pilkington, Johnny Radar, Elizabeth James, Martin Goodson, Tom Oldham, Reena Makwanna, Richard Sanderson, Danielle Sutcliffe, Steven Barrett and those of you I have doubtless forgotten. Thank you, I could not have done it without you.

There is a bibliography at the back of this book, but writing and researching London's urban legends would have been far harder and a lot less fun without the writings of Rodney Dale, Jan Harold Brunvand, Michael Goss, James Hayward,

Steve Roud, Antony Clayton and Barbara and David Mikkelson, as well as the editors, writers and contributors of the *Fortean Times*, *Magonia* magazine and the Folklore Society Newsletter. Thank you, thank you, thank you!

I owe a debt of gratitude to the London Metropolitan Archive, Royal Society of Architects Archive, the British Library and British Newspaper Library, Bishopsgate Institute Library and Archive, Guildhall Library and Transport for London's Corporate Archives, as well as Clare Norman at Lidl public relations, Tom Artrocker, Jo Tanner at Us Ltd and the Museum of London archaeology department for their patience.

Thank you to the London Fortean Society, the London Cryptozoology Club and the South East London Folklore Society who have let me indulge my obsession for these topics in public.

INTRODUCTION

....

Ghost and other horror stories, political and social commentaries, dirty jokes (hundreds of them!), black humours tales, episodes of revenge, and topical pieces which rely on the audience's shared reaction to AIDS, nuclear warfare, foreigners, etc.

◆

Michael Goss answers his question 'What are urban legends about?' in the article 'Legends for Our Time' in the July 1987 issue of The Unknown.

....

THIS IS A book about urban legends and London. The brief for the book is a brilliant one: collect, share and attempt to interpret the funny, scary, filthy and bizarre contemporary legends weaving their way through everyday London life. I hope to have written a book that is about London and urban legends, as well as how they relate to each other. This is a book of London tales that finds strange stories and lost and bizarre truths amongst the folklore. This is a book that looks at urban legends using the capital city of the United Kingdom as a frame whilst not neglecting their ability to travel anywhere there are people, and their talent for adapting very quickly to their environment. It is true that urban legends are universal rather than local, but one way urban legends thrive is by their immediacy: they attach themselves to people and places. It is also true that the temperament of tale-tellers, their audience and the land-scape they share shapes their legendary life. Some of the stories in this book are as synonymous with London as mash and liquor with your pie, as people who talk all the way through gigs and having to queue for the swings in the playground. If you are not familiar with the city, this book is a strange introduction, but it can still show you around. You would be just as likely to find yourself standing over a possible plague pit or under a forgotten church gargoyle as in the middle of Trafalgar Square or outside Buckingham Palace. Ideas about London are far more widely spread than ones on urban legends, so I shall spend a few more pages introducing those. But fear not, the city runs through this entire book.

Urban myths are thought of as untrue stories pretending to be true, which they partly are, but I have recently heard many a fallacy or falsehood being denounced as being merely an urban myth. This is not true: there is always some level of narrative within an urban myth or legend. I may have stretched the meaning myself here to include moral panics, delusions and hoaxes, but each of these carries a story within them or are delivered by a fear or belief with a narrative. Urban myths are the stories told by ordinary people to entertain and to communicate a truth, opinion or prejudice through a story. Just as fairy tales explain the dangers of going into the woods at night, tell stories of kings or princesses going to a market in disguise, or why a local rock looks a certain shape, an urban myth will explain the dangers of using the London underground at night, tells a story of a celebrity or princess going to a local pub or bar, or describes why a building or statue is a certain shape. Other urban legends are a mad idea that rocket through the public consciousness, a story just plausible enough to spread: rioters releasing animals from London Zoo; a green patch of land in an overcrowded city lying empty because it hides a deadly secret. Others are even more vague, like the idea that big cats (pumas and panthers) have escaped their rich owners or zoos, and prowl the edges of the city; that urban fox hunts are something that may be useful and real.

There is a mystery to these myths. I have not set out to solve these mysteries, but to offer (hopefully) informed suggestions as to how and why they came to be.

✧ Origin of Myths ✧

In keeping with something as nebulous as urban myths, the origins of the phrase, along with the term urban legend, are not straightforward. Many believe that the American professor and writer Jan Harold Brunvald coined the phrase 'urban legend', and his books certainly helped popularise the phrase, but the credit could also go to American folklorist, Richard Dorson, who apparently used it in a 1968 essay 'Legends and Tall Tales' (in *Our Living Traditions*, edited by Tristram P. Coffin). Dorson is the earliest citation in the *Oxford English Dictionary*, but this does not make him the man who minted the phrase. Dorson used it himself in a 1962 article. Researching the origin in *Foaftale News*, Charles Clay Doyle and Lara Renee Knight found a *New York Times* article from 6 December 1925 regarding Europe's population growth: 'Around the subject of population there has been a growth of popular legend hard to remove. Great Britain illustrates the urban legend.' This described a myth of urban life: that it is unhealthy and squalid compared to rural living and is not used to describe contemporary legends and myths. The phrase is old, has multiple uses and its roots are hard to uncover.

Reading Michael Goss's article in the June 1987 small digest magazine *The Unknown*, the main aspect of urban myths that first captured my imagination was the idea that stories could migrate and adapt themselves as they travel. It was the first time I imagined stories with a life beyond their author. One could read a book written by a deceased writer, but it would still be in their book.

But what if the writer was gone, the books, films and songs were forgotten, but somehow their story lived on and found an ever-changing existence travelling around the world?

I began reading magazines like *The Unexplained* and *The Unknown* as a precocious pre-adolescent looking for aliens stepping out of UFOs, ghosts drawing themselves out of ancient wallpaper and monsters lurking in the misty night but found something far more humane and fascinating that could contain all of these gaudy wonders. My fascination with the paranormal was enlarged and refined. Years later I was lucky enough to catch Jan Harold Brunvald speak at the *Fortean Times* gathering, the UnConvention, which reignited my interest.

When American psychologist F.C. Bartlett experimented with how stories change through retelling, his conclusions rang true for urban myths. Details difficult to repeat were smoothed out, and in Bartlett's test story, 'canoes' became 'boats' and 'bush-cats' became 'cats'. Any unusual parts of the story begin to be rationalised and morals formed either through this process or as a reason for telling the story. The experiment was short and contained to a small peergroup, while urban legends are feral and free, but it makes sense that stories survive, not just because they are entertaining but because they carry a central lesson or meaning.

As I have already said, the term urban myth and legend is now used to describe contemporary folk stories. One problem raised by this is that where there are gatherings of people, there are legends, myths and folklore; and London has been an urban environment for around two thousand years. If we were to find a story told by the Romans about a part of London life, would that be an urban myth? Classical myths and legends are often of gods, heroes and supernatural creatures, but urban myths also trouble themselves with royalty and celebrities and wander into the supernatural and paranormal to include ghosts, monsters and stories of miracles. They are not always stories of the common folk.

Other names have been suggested for these tales: Rodney Dale arguably wrote the first acknowledged urban myth book, without using the term, in 1972; *The Tumour in the Whale* suggested the phrase 'whale tumours', inspired by stories of rationing era whale meat being eaten as a substitute for beef, with its unusual status confirmed with wobbly growths. The phrase did not catch on, but Dale did bring together the phrase 'friend-of-a-friend' and abbreviate it to 'foaf' in order to describe the ever-apocryphal source of an urban myth. David J. Jacobson, in his 1948 book *The Affairs of Dame Rumour,* and Sir Basil Thomson, in his 1922 book *Queer People,* both encountered and understood the source of a story as always being just beyond arms' length – they are quoted later in this book describing the process in more depth. Another good term for these stories is the Swedish *vandresagn*, meaning 'wandering legends' that travel by people sharing stories. Sharing stories is as old as humanity and is still a powerful way for us to express our feelings and innermost thoughts, from epics to emails and campfires to Kindles.

Scott Wood, 2013

LONDON PHRASE AND FABLE

But the truth is this is not how London is apprehended. It is divided into chapters, the chapters into scenes, the scenes into sentences; it opens to you like a series of rooms, door, passage, door.

♦

Anna Quindlen, Imagined London

WHY DO WE use that phrase? Why is that statue so strange? Why is that big stone there? Where is that actual place?

There is often a story to answer questions like this about a local landmark. It is as if a large physical object or popular idea deserves to have a neat narrative fixed to it. Once you start examining the origins of a myth or phrase, you can be led down strange alleys and cul-de-sacs chasing old stories and ideas. Things can become confused and leave your thoughts in some disarray or, to use the particularly apt phrase, 'at sixes and sevens'.

The phrase 'at sixes and sevens' is said to have a London origin and refers to a feud between the Merchant Taylors and Merchant Skinners livery companies. Both were founded in the City of London around the same time, so they argued about who should come sixth and who should come seventh in the Order of Precedence, a list of London livery companies organised by age collected from 1515.

'To fall off the wagon' means to succumb to the temptation of alcohol; to be on the wagon is to not drink, so to fall off is to start drinking again. One possible origin of this saying, much-loved on *The Robert Elms Show* on BBC London Radio, is from when prisoners were taken from Newgate Prison to Tyburn to be hanged. Halfway to their execution there would be a stop where the condemned could have a last drink. One origin of this tradition could be that a 'cup of charity' was bequeathed by Queen Matilda (wife of Henry I). The prisoner would get off the wagon at a tavern at St-Giles-in-the-Fields and have a pint of ale in the cup, and then get back on the wagon to go to Tyburn. He would never drink again. Another version, collected by Snopes, has the last stop at Marble Arch, right by the site of the gallows. A retelling from the Nursery Rhymes: Lyrics, Origins and History website puts a line of dialogue into the story. If the prisoner was offered a second drink, the guard would say, 'No, he's on the wagon.' If they had friends in the crowd they would, perhaps, be pulled off the wagon and rescued. This is falling off the wagon.

The word 'tawdry', which means something that is cheap, low quality and maybe makes you a bit sad to give or receive as a gift, also has its origins in London. St Ethelreda's Church on Ely Place, London's oldest Catholic place of worship, is near London's diamond and jewellery centre, Hatton Garden. I was told by a trustworthy source, a Blue Badge guide no less, that the church gave us the word from the poorer quality trinkets from the area which was said to be a bit 'St Audrey', another version of the name Ethelreda.

All of these phrases make sense on their own, hermetically sealed in their own story. Outside of these are far different possible origins. 'At sixes and sevens' bumbles all the way back to the Old Testament with 'six, yea, seven', meaning an indefinite number and so is unknown and confusing. In the *Book of Job* is the line that God 'shall deliver thee in six troubles, yea in seven', and it is likely that the Bible has more influence over popular culture than London's livery companies and their lore. Another biblical origin is the story of an error in the King James Bible, in which the sixth commandment is 'Thou Shalt Not Kill' and the seventh 'Thou Shalt Not Commit Adultery'. In the Septuagint version, not committing adultery comes in sixth and the seventh is 'Thou Shalt Not Steal'. Which puts bible scholars at sixes and sevens. Another non-biblical origin is from the French game played with dice called Hazard, where six and seven are the most hazardous numbers to shoot for and anyone attempting it is thought to be careless or confused.

Does tawdry come from St Ethelreda? Perhaps, but not the one in London. St Ethelreda's sits within Ely Place, the site of the palace for the Bishop of Cambridge, and the church started life as the palace's private chapel. An earlier version is that the word comes from St Audrey lace sold on at the fair of St Audrey on the Isle of Ely in Cambridgeshire.

The phrases 'on the wagon' and 'fall off the wagon' evolved probably not along the streets between Newgate and Tyburn but in America. The earliest known version appeared in the 1901 book *Mrs Wiggs of the Cabbage Patch*, the phrase referring to the water wagons used in America to dampen down dusty roads. The American Temperance movement formed the phrase to describe someone who is not drinking. They felt so strongly about the sinfulness of alcohol that they would rather drink water from the water wagon than let alcohol pass their lips, although now I write it down this explanation sounds just as implausible as the Tyburn theory. The excellent online resource, Snopes, suggests that 'on the wagon' is a derivation of 'following the bandwagon'. The bandwagon is a phrase coined, as far as we know, by the American showman P.T. Barnum to describe what his shows travelled around in, and 'to jump on the bandwagon' means to follow or join the fair. The word only goes back as far as the nineteenth century, with 'on the wagon' still coming to us from the members of the Temperance movement. Any connection to the journey to Tyburn was almost certainly retro-fitted in the twentieth or twenty-first century as speculation made story, or by joining the dots of distance and unrelated ideas to make a pleasing narrative pattern. We can't help but do it; it's impossible for us just to shrug and say 'I don't know' when wondering about such a thing, so we write stories to explain the mysterious origins of phrase and fables.

THE HIDDEN INSULT

....

*I like the idea of infiltrating an area that is
not really exposed to me or my work.*

✦

Alexander McQueen

....

✧ Royally Rude ✧

When London-based fashion designer Alexander McQueen was
found dead on 11 February 2010, the response was one of shock
and grief. His suicide was all over the media and the loss was felt
by even the scruffiest of Londoners.

Remembering him in the 2010 obituaries in the 12 December
edition of the *Observer*, Harriet Quick, fashion features director
at *Vogue*, described his collections as 'wildly imaginative' whilst
McQueen was a 'shy, sensitive man'. Quick suggested that a
McQueen fashion show had such power it could actually affect

nature, remembering that 'his shows were frequently accompanied by freak weather', and she describes driving through a hurricane to see a show in New York in 2000. In past times and other lands the sky threatens at war, disaster or the death of a monarch or beloved leader. Alexander McQueen only needed to showcase some expensive clothes that most people could not wear for storms to descend.

Another reason that McQueen was so loved was his background as a working-class east London boy who got to the top of fashion because of his skill, talent and vision. During the remembrance for him in the media a story emerged about a prank McQueen had pulled whilst an apprentice at Savile Row tailors Gieves & Hawkes. The young designer found himself making a jacket (or suit) for the Prince of Wales and could not resist the temptation to put a message within the lining of the jacket. The Radio 4 obituary show *Last Word* broadcast on 14 February 2010 described the story of McQueen writing 'McQueen was here' in the royal jacket as apocryphal, and his BBC online obituary recounts the story but puts a 'reportedly' ahead of it. Another version, alluded to on the London Design Museum website, is that McQueen actually wrote 'I am a c★★★' inside Prince Charles' suit. This is much celebrated on the internet, and in the 'Dressed to Thrill' column of the *New Yorker* on 16 May 2011, Judith Thurman moved the scene of the crime to McQueen's first apprenticeship at Anderson & Sheppherd and reported that the tailors recalled every jacket made for Prince Charles because of the alledged message.

* * *

These stories celebrate McQueen as an *enfant terrible* of the fashion world, slyly calling the establishment that fed him a c★★★. Like the world of artists and rock stars, the world of fashion designers is never knowingly under-mythologised and such a story feeds the myth. The swearword jacket story echoes another urban legend I heard about a car belonging to the Queen. Back in the early 1990s, I was working in a warehouse and heard a story in the staff canteen (a comfier and earlier version of the work water cooler as a place to share stories). One car – maybe more than one Rolls-Royce – constructed for the Queen had pornographic magazines secretly hidden in the body work. As well as being another rumour of royalty unwittingly carrying around obscenities, this urban legend also nods to a legend about the cars themselves. Rolls-Royce cars often glided through the popular imagination in the 1970s and '80s and, as with anything, stories followed in their wake. The 'Rolls of legend,' wrote Rodney Dale in *The Tumour in the Whale*, 'has a sealed bonnet, which must never be opened except at the factory.' Perhaps knowing this legend inspired some factory workers to leave something inside the monarch's car.

There is a more fully formed, muscular American version of the car urban legend picked up by Jan Harold Brunvand in his book *The Choking Doberman and Other 'New' Urban Legends*. It literally delivers the message of class war in the narrative. A 'wealthy professional man' has ordered a new Cadillac, which is perfect except for a persistent rattling sound when the car is driven, particularly over railway tracks or a bumpy street. After a number of check-ups, the man has the car deconstructed piece by piece and a bottle or tin can, hidden in the body work, is found to be the culprit. Within the recepticle there is an insulting note that reads 'You rich SOB – so you finally found the rattle!'

✧ Royalty to Celebrity ✧

The Prince of Wales is not the only affluent jacket wearer to be secretly insulted by a sly tailor. *Popbitch*, the celebrity gossip newsletter and website, told the story in its 2 July 2009 email of footballer Joe Cole's 'beautiful bespoke suit for his wedding'. Cole had recently left West Ham to join Chelsea, and 'someone involved in stitching up the suit' was a West Ham supporter. Knowing the suit was for Cole, the supporter chalked a full West Ham insignia on the lining and 'a few choice words', including 'Judas'.

Football folklore has its own traditions of hidden insults. Scottish memorabilia and tartan scarves can be found under the dugouts and turf of the new Wembley stadium, left at the heart of English football by Scottish construction workers. Outside of London, a similar story is told of the construction of Southampton's new football ground, with some of the builders supporting local rivals Portsmouth. Three football shirts are buried beneath the turf, inscribed bricks are buried in the foundations and seeds were planted in the centre circle which would have, at some point, sprouted to spell out 'Pompey', Portsmouth's nickname. The seed story reminds me of another legend I have heard, set during and after the Second World War, which takes us from football fans to Nazis. A German prisoner of war distinguished himself as a gardener at the English manor house where he had been put to work. The war ended and the time came for the POW to return home, and it was apparently with much sadness that he parted company with the people of the manor house. This sadness was jarred the following spring when a swastika of daffodils sprouted up on the lawn. As we shall see regularly throughout this book, urban legends, like flowers, are often seeded from older growths.

The hidden insult has travelled from royalty to celebrity. This is not surprising considering pop stars, sport stars and television personalities are our newest form of rich aristocracy and are, at present, even more in the public eye than royalty. In the 1990s the rising stars of the Britpop movement – Blur and Oasis – developed a bitter rivalry, sparked off, partly (these things are messy), by Blur releasing the single 'Country House' on the same day (14 August 1995) as Oasis's single 'Roll With It'. Egged on by the media, the race to No. 1 became a class war between the northern working-class lads of Oasis and the southern, middle-class art students of Blur, which peaked with Oasis's songwriter Noel Gallagher wishing death by AIDS on Blur's lead singer Damon Albarn. Once again we refer to the *Popbitch* newsletter, this time from 21 August 2009. It contained the story of Oasis buying a vintage EMI TG mixing desk from a studio in Australia. A 'famous record producer' heard the band were buying it and carved the name of their rivals Blur on the inside of it. Popbitch reported that the producer said: 'He's always wondered if the Gallaghers ever found his handiwork.'

Back in London, and hidden insults are not only aimed at football teams but whole sporting events. On 28 February 2012, the 150-day mark before the start of the London Olympics, 37ft high, 82ft wide Olympic rings were floated up the Thames. These iconic symbols were to be paraded and displayed all around London to herald the Olympics, at a reported cost of £3.2 million. This generated comments from within London of the cost when the city, along with the rest of Great Britain, was suffering from unemployment, crime and rioting, pay cuts, pay freezes and funding cuts to the arts and libraries. The fanfare of the Olympics and its expense seemed garish and crude in comparison. 'There were better things to have spent this money on,' said the Green Party's 2012 mayoral candidate Jenny Jones. This attitude remained until Danny Boyle's opening ceremony, and a lot of talented Britons achieving medals finally won over even the curmudgeonliest of taxpayers. So, perhaps it was not surprising that the 22 March 2012 edition of *Popbitch* had the following story: 'We're told that there's something special about one of the rings. Someone involved in their construction had a bit of a downer on the whole Olympics in London thing. So he took a shit inside one of the rings. And then had it welded shut.'

✧ Finding the Hidden Insult ✧

To be completely fair to *Popbitch*, they are not some golly-gosh, typo-ridden vacuous scandal rag. The newsletter often writes intelligently about the nature of celebrity and of the media, and they have a passion for music that steps outside the present pop charts. When repeating these urban legends, they are frequently in the company of the BBC, the *Guardian* and the Design Museum websites. *Popbitch* have shown themselves to be urban legend savvy when repeating the story of the rich premiership footballer paying off a couple's mortgage so he could take their booking for the wedding venue of his choice. 'It's one of the oldest shaggy dog stories going', they wrote in their 12 April 2012 newsletter before going on to reference an old legend of a female actor and television personality famous for doing on someone's chest, or onto a glass-topped coffee table, what some disgruntled person did into one of the giant Olympic rings. The next week they even produced a desperate email saying the children of the celebrity have 'worked their arses off' to keep her off the internet for fear that she might stumble across the mortifying rumour.

Seeking the hidden insult may provoke similar responses: who does one ask about a rumoured swearword or stool hidden in a public place or on the back of a public figure? I have wondered about contacting Clarence House, the seat for the Prince of Wales, but perhaps they too are working very hard to keep this rumour away from his royal ears. I would not wish to be instrumental in His Royal Highness glaring at his old jackets as his butler dresses him.

The McQueen story's popularity after the designer's death prompted his old company Anderson & Sheppard to issue a statement about the rumour on their blog. It denied the possibility of McQueen writing an insult into a suit or jacket:

Alexander McQueen joined here in 1984 or 1985. He didn't have an introduction I don't think, he just came in to apply in person. The firm's policy at the time was to take young people who had not been to college as they were easier to train. Sixteen was a typical age for apprentices joining the firm.

He worked under a tailor called Cornelius O'Callaghan – one of the best coatmakers that the firm had. Cornelius was known as Con, and was the strictest tailor at the firm. He checked his apprentices' work thoroughly. Despite rumours that things were scribbled inside the lining of a coat for Prince Charles, Con wouldn't have permitted that. And in fact the coat was recalled and checked after the story came out – nothing was found.

The story of the insulting objects hidden inside the Queen's car is true. The car was a Jaguar rather than a Rolls-Royce, and pornographic magazines and a swastika were found behind a seat panel when the car was being bomb-proofed. These, perhaps, were the most offensive things the prankster could think of, as are all of the hidden insults discussed. Even a football shirt hidden in the foundations of a rival's grounds can be viewed as a deadly insult. Stories appeared in the press in June 2001, and one in the *Buckingham Post* dated 14 June also referenced the McQueen story as 'McQueen Woz Ere' rather than 'was here'.

An unnamed Jaguar employee is quoted as saying; 'It is one of those old traditions where people used to write things behind the seat panel of cars and they were never discovered unless there was an accident. But on this occasion it was not very funny.' The discovery of the magazines and swastika resulted in the dismissal of an unnamed worker. Another unnamed source at the *Coventry Evening Telegraph* of 13 June 2001 described the insult as a regular prank by apprentices: 'I have never understood if it's for good luck or what, but the person knows the owner of the car will never see it. This one came to light, but normally they never do.'

The story of McQueen's Savile Row prank is set in his early days, perhaps during his apprenticeship at Anderson & Sheppard. Apprentices have rituals and rites and, by their nature, apprentices are young and irreverent. Is there a tradition, particularly when producing something like a car or jacket for rich customers, of hiding something offensive within it?

Unlike the Queen's car, the McQueen story does not have any evidence for it so far. The stories have generally been passed on informally. The *Daily Telegraph*, writing enthusiastically about Prince Charles' fashion sense on 13 June 2012, claimed that the original was written in the lining of an overcoat by McQueen at Anderson & Sheppard, while a 2011 feature on the *Vogue* website, dated 11 May 2011, puts the scene of the fashion crime at Gieves & Hawkes, stating that McQueen was embroidering a suit, not making a coat. I have not been able to find a definitive interview with Alexander McQueen in which he states that there is any truth to the rumour. It does not seem like anyone else is referring back to an original article either, as the versions vary so much. There may be one out there somewhere, but the popularity of the myth of this hidden insult is because it perfectly encapsulates who Alexander McQueen was and how he did things.

It is always the underdog that leaves the insult, never a privileged bully hiding a 'kick me' sign on the back of an employee or minion. Even the Oasis *v.* Blur story relates to a time when middle-class Blur were the chart underdogs to the 'champagne supernova' of Oasis's success. Oasis' album at the time '(What's the Story) Morning Glory' spent ten weeks at No. 1 and sold 16 million copies. Apparently, it was not a member of Blur who hid the message in the desk but a studio producer.

Where is the reality in this? Urban myths often create more questions the deeper you look into them, but each question leads to a truth about our own selves and fears even if they lead away from any actual event. Is the hidden insult regularly concealed on the property of the prosperous by an insubordinate? By its very nature it is hard to tell. There is something known as 'ostentation in folklore'. This describes people hearing a folk story or urban legend and, by copying it, making the story actually real. Had stories of the Queen's car and Prince Charles' jacket inspired a cheeky studio worker and a fed-up artist constructing a giant Olympic monument? And who wants to open up these objects and check?

THE QUEEN'S HEAD AND THE KRAYS' ARMS

*Up the stairs to the balcony where King Edward VII,
so the foreman told me, liked to have his chair to watch
the dancers on the floor below.*

✦

Geoffrey Fletcher, The London Nobody Knows

LONDON IS A city riddled with royalty, with statues of monarchs popping up in all manner of unexpected places (*See* 'The Suicidal Sculptor' p. 68 and 'The Misadventures of Brandy Nan' p. 85 for more on those) and the hulking presence of Buckingham Palace at the edge of Green Park is a reminder of our present royal incumbents. From newspapers we know what the younger royals (mostly Prince Harry) like to get up to in the evening, but what about the Queen herself? How does she occupy herself when off duty?

The general idea, I think, is of Her Majesty sitting on a gilded seat watching *EastEnders* with Prince Philip muttering next to her in his dressing gown. Another suggestion, picked up by Rodney Dale in *The Tumour in the Whale*, came from a friend-of-a-friend who knew an under-footman at Buckingham Palace who said there is a secret side door and that late at night the Queen emerges and secretly goes window shopping around Piccadilly, Bond Street and Oxford Street.

Stories of royals among us are as old as England itself, and I'm sure everyone around my age remembers the Ladybird book with the image of King Alfred burning the cakes (or loaves) he was asked to mind by a peasant woman. The peasant woman scolded the incompetent kitchen help, without realising it was the king. Alfred was in disguise after fleeing to the Somerset Levels to hide from the Danes.

A more recent rumour was of the myth-magnet Diana, Princess of Wales sneaking out of Kensington Palace in a baseball cap and shades to visit the local newsagent, or simply walk along the high street unharassed. Other word-of-mouth stories had her going out clubbing in a dark wig. In his book *A Royal Duty* Paul Burrell described buying a long, dark wig and large glasses so that Diana could have a night out in Ronnie Scott's Jazz Club in Soho. She even chatted up the man standing next to her in the queue who, she said to Burrell, didn't have a clue who she was.

Paul Burrell's role as the only man Diana trusted makes these stories difficult to verify and there is a whiff of myth about them. The meaning of them, like the Queen going window shopping, is handily given to us by Diana, marvelling at the freedom of disguise, when she said, 'I can be me in a public place!'

Alfred was in isolation and pondering his fate when the cakes burnt, like Robert the Bruce when he was inspired by a tenacious spider. His story, unlike Diana and Queen Elizabeth's, shows how different he was to ordinary citizens; he was pondering the fate of his nation as the baked goods burned, while the twentieth-century tales suggest that royalty can yearn for something that resembles normal life. Another story of royal otherness, as well as enforcing the ancient advice of always being polite to strangers, is of King James and the tinker. It's a ballad that tells of the king slipping his retinue whilst hunting to go 'in hope of some pass time'. Like a lot of unsupervised men (and incognito Princesses of Wales) with time on their hands, James went to an alehouse and fell into conversation with a tinker over a beer or two. After a while the tinker let slip that he'd heard the king was in the forest, so James got him to jump up on his horse so they could find him. They found James's entourage, and the tinker asked which one was the king. James said it was the only one with a hat on, which was he, and the poor tinker fell to his knees to beg for forgiveness. The king knighted his new drinking buddy, who kept his sack of tinker-tools hanging up in his new, grand hall. The location of the story varies; some claim it is Enfield in north London, where there is a King and Tinker pub that commemorates the story if not any actual event. Norwood in Surrey also claims the story, and there are other, similar stories told about different monarchs in Tamworth and Mansfield.

A recurring theme with these legends is that celebrity increasingly replaces royalty as the subject of the story. When the eccentric and much-loved New Cross pub, the Montague Arms, closed in early 2012, the local blog 'Transpontine' asked for readers' reminiscences of nights and events there. The pub was famous for the blind keyboard player who played cover versions to bemused locals, and coach parties on their way in or out of London. Pete, the keyboard player, would invite members of the audience (including this author) up on stage to sing. One response to Transpontine's request began at this point and was told to one contributor by the pub's former barman, Stan: 'This funny fellah wearing white gloves took to the key board and played the most amazing tunes – 'twas like magic running through his fingertips…'

Who was it? None other than Mr Michael Jackson!

✧ Criminal Tourism ✧

Michael Jackson and Ronnie and Reggie Kray may not have too many things in common, but all three were said to have visited the Montague Arms. The visit, like the description of a similar visit by the gangsters to Peter Cook's club The Establishment, treats their appearance as almost a celebrity endorsement rather than a demand for money.

London's most famous criminals, from Dick Turpin to the Kray twins, have taken on a legendary status different to the rest of the stories in this book. They are folk heroes who are celebrated for their rough individuality and rule-breaking, and are even thought to be protectors of the common man. One warm Friday night in July 2012, I passed the bus stop opposite Shoreditch Town Hall and a woman, appalled by the hipsters and trendies swaggering past her along this East End street, shouted: 'If only the Krays were still here. They'd sort this out!' Murdering, bully gangsters are now the protectors of the common people who would keep the fey and pretentious out of east London, a vigilante fashion and lifestyle police. I think the attraction to organised criminals like the Krays, the Richardsons and Dick Turpin is that they live successfully by their own rules and not according to the limitations of bureaucracy, government or corporate values. It is imagined that they then become an informal sheriff of their area, not tolerating any crime other than their own.

Whilst not as popular as nearby Jack the Ripper tours, Kray tours have been written so visitors can see the sights of their crime spree. The Blind Beggar pub in Bethnal Green is where Ronnie Kray murdered rival gangster George Cornell. Tourists regularly arrive, looking for the bullet holes from the murder. They should be directed to the Magdela pub on South Hill Park near Hampstead Heath station. Here, a drunk Ruth Ellis shot her boyfriend David Blakely on 10 April 1955 as he left the pub, famously making herself the last woman to be executed in Britain. The four or five bullet holes have been visible since and are regularly referred to in many pub guides. Pubs are, of course, commercial enterprises and keen to use any means to bring people to the site. This could be a ghost, an historical arte-fact or a story with the evidence for all to see, like a bullet hole, a modern version of the indelible bloodstain that testifies to an ancient murder.

The holes from Ellis' gun are said to be visible in the white wall of the pub and a plaque was hung by them, explaining what the pock-marks on the building are. The plaque has since been stolen or removed; it got the year of the murder wrong, saying that Blakely was shot in 1954. It has been suggested that these marks were enhanced by a previous landlady and may not be linked to the murder at all.

Crime tourism is not new in London. Dick Turpin is one character who seemed to drink and take shelter in pretty much every pub across London except the ones Claude Duval, the Dandy Highwayman, drank in. The London pub most closely associated with Dick Turpin is the Spaniards Inn, which once boasted knives and forks used by him, as well as a small window where the highwayman could be aided and abetted by pub staff who would pass him food, money and drink while he was still in his saddle. *Old and New London* describes the Coach and Horses pub in Hockley in the Hole, now Ray Street, where a valise marked 'R. Turpin' was found in the cellars along with blank keys used for lock-breaking. Also at the Coach and Horses, still on Ray Street and a backstreet, was said to be a passage from the pub cellar that lead out to the banks of the Fleet river which was used by highwaymen or, as the book calls them, 'minions of the moon'. Turpin also left another unholy relic, a pistol engraved with 'Dick's Friend' in the rafters of the Anchor Inn in Shepperton and another within the walls of Ye Old King's Head in Chigwell.

✧ Tunnel Visions ✧

There are countless pubs that claim a link to Dick Turpin, but the Dick they are referring to is the romantic, fictional figure and not the actual Richard Turpin, a thuggish burglar and thief. Like the Ellis shooting, the Old Red Lion pub on Whitechapel High Street has a plaque stating 'This is the Old Red Lion where Dick Turpin shot Tom King' after the murder committed here on 1 May 1737. Inside the pub was another plaque with the following inscription: 'It was in the yard of this house that Dick Turpin shot Tom King. Turpin had been traced by the horse to this inn, together with Matthew and Robert King, birds of like feather, by the Bow Street Runners.'

Antony Clayton in *Folklore of London* says of this plague: 'Apart from the fact that it was Matthew King who was shot, that Matthew's brother's name was John and not Robert and that the Bow Street Runners were founded in 1750, after Turpin's death, this sign was accurate.'

Other London pubs claiming a link to Turpin include the Spotted Dog on Upton Lane, and the Black Lion on Plaistow High Street, with tunnels extending 'over half a mile to emerge very close to Upton Park football ground', which Turpin would scuttle down after stabling Black Bess. Chigwell's Old King's Head has a tunnel that Turpin used to escape from the cellars, presumably after stashing his guns in the wall (Turpin did foolishly risk incriminating himself by signing his equipment). Turpin hid in the Globe Tavern on Bow Street for three days, and the temptation of this legend couldn't resist having him being pursued again by the non-existent Bow Street Runners.

Tunnels for Turpin's escape and stables for Black Bess's rest multiply as often as someone thinks of Turpin or visits an old pub for a drink. There were many more criminals and gangsters in London than the Krays, Richardsons and Dick Turpin, but the further the past gets, and the more romanticised these criminals become, it will be the most famous names that will live on in legend. By 2113 there will pubs called 'The Reggie Kray' or 'The Jack the Ripper' in the East End that will show places these folk heroes killed, or hid, or escaped down a secret tunnel.

Highwaymen are not the only historical celebrities to use secret tunnels, however. Royalty and aristocracy had the means to construct tunnels to cover their clandestine indulgences.

Legends of tunnels and the famous are insistent things that cannot help but insinuate themselves into a discovery. The Argyll Arms on Argyll Street is named after the Duke of Argyll. 'Rumour has it', the pub's website says, 'that a secret tunnel once connected the pub to the duke's mansion.' When staff at Wimbledon Park Golf Club discovered a tunnel in February 2012 the newspaper headline was 'Mysterious tunnels could link golf course with Henry VIII's Wimbledon home', though I think Henry was more a hunting, archery and wrestling man. His daughter, Elizabeth I, shimmied out of the Tower of London during her incarceration in 1554 to take wine in the nearby, but now long-gone, Tiger Tavern. She is also said to have stopped at the Tiger for a drink before heading to Tilbury to speak with the troops before they met the Spanish Armada, and to have used a secret passage that runs from the Old Queen's Head pub in Islington to Canonbury Tower to meet in secret with the Earl of Essex; not that Essex ever lived in Canonbury Tower.

Pubs are public places, a neutral ground with alcohol and comfy chairs and so are ideal places to meet old friends and new people. If urban legend is to be believed, then the great and good of London history were just as keen on a liaison in the pub as highwaymen and gangsters. The Nell of Old Drury has a secret passage running under the road which Charles II used to visit Nell Gwynne. The pub wasn't named after her then, being known at the time as The Lamb. The Red Lion at No. 23 Crown Passage has a tunnel, according to legend, running to No. 79 Pall Mall which Nell used to meet Charles in the pub. When Antony Clayton, an expert on underground London, inquired with the landlady in 2007, he was told of two doors in the cellar facing south in the direction of Pall Mall. (Are they 'his' and 'hers'?) When the Pindar of Wakefield on Gray's Inn Road – now Water Rats – was rebuilt in 1878, an underground tunnel was found heading in the direction of Bagnigge Wells, a pleasure garden where Nell and Charles met up. I've heard speculation that nearly every pub in London with the name Nelson in it was either a place Nelson and Emma Hamilton met, or was started by a wounded sailor pensioned out of the Napoleonic Wars with enough money to start a pub. Attentions in the pub are not always welcome: there is a story of Shakespeare being a regular at the George Inn on Borough High Street and catching the attention of a barmaid. One day Will was in the pub with the keys to the Globe on his person, when the barmaid grabbed the keys and placed them in her cleavage along with the key to her own room, asking the bard which set he desired.

When not meeting for a date in an inn or tavern, the famous did enjoy a drink. Charles Dickens had a reputation for being a furious drinker and countless pubs claim him as a regular, as they do Dr Johnson. Several pubs claim that Christopher Wren ordered them built in order to water the workers building St Paul's Cathedral: amongst those claiming this association are The Salutation on Newgate Street, now gone, and the Old Bell on Fleet Street. Ye Old Watling on Watling Street also claims to have been built for St Paul's workers as well as having an upstairs room in which Wren worked during the project.

Another result of a royal visit is an ordinary place being given a special licence. In the rural areas this could be a passing king with a thirst changing a blacksmiths into a pub so he could get a drink. In London the most famous version is the Castle on Cowcross Street becoming a pawnbroker after George IV found himself at a cock fight at nearby Hockley-in-the-Hole without any cash. The Castle was the nearest pub, so he went in to borrow money from the landlord, using a watch as a deposit. The landlord did not recognise the royal but agreed nonetheless and George won the next bet, redeemed his watch and granted a Royal Warrant to the pub to also trade as a pawnbroker. Three brass balls still hang in the pub as a memorial and a large painting commemorates the event inside. There is another London story of a monarch granting a drinking establishment a special licence after a favour. When Edward III had run out of money, he borrowed some from several City Vintners. Instead of repaying them, he granted them the right to sell wine without a licence. This is why the Boot and Flogger wine bar, tucked down Redcross Way in Borough, can sell wine without a licence: it is owned by the Freemen of the Vintners Company.

It goes without saying that all of these stories should be taken with a fair amount of salt, the most artery hardening one being the story I stumbled upon, saying that the Blind Beggar pub in Bethnal Green, of Kray infamy, was named after the Edinburgh bodysnatcher William Hare who, after getting William Burke executed, found himself in Limehouse where he was thrown into the lime pits. Blinded, he migrated to Bethnal Green to become the famous beggar. The generally agreed story of the Blind Beggar is that he was Henry de Montfort, son of Simon de Montfort, who had been defeated by the son of Henry III, Prince Edward, at the battle of Evesham. Wounded and blind from the battle, Henry lived in disguise as the Blind Beggar of Bethnal Green to escape the attention of Edward, who was now King Edward I. According to this legend the Blind Beggar is another aristocrat incognito amongst ordinary Londoners.

These stories have plenty of meaning; they remind us of the biblical teaching of entertaining strangers as they may be angels or royalty in disguise, and that the lives of the rich, famous and infamous are like ours. They still drink and have sex, and yet are different; they need to build secret tunnels to go and do it. They, like saints and ghosts, bring a mysterious aura to a location, be it a cosy old pub or an unremarkable boozer with a claim to fame. In a city that has always enjoyed the money of tourists and travellers, such a claim or artefact can draw people to a location and feed urban legends for centuries afterwards.

THE GENITALS
OF LONDON

4

*To Pee or Not to Pee: An Overview of Electricity Related Deaths,
and Examination of the Question of Whether Peeing on the
Third Rail Can Kill*

◆

*PowerPoint presentation, medical examiner's
office in Cook County, Illinois*

THERE ARE FEW things less socially acceptable than a
stray penis. The penis is chiefly for having sex and urinating, two things that are unacceptable in public. For this
reason, no doubt, it is the penis that protrudes into a number of
London urban legends, demonstrating the ongoing fascination
and awkwardness people feel about it.

So pity the man in the following legend collected by Rodney
Dale and written up for his book *The Tumour in the Whale*.
A man rushes into the saloon bar of a City of London pub, puts

his hat and briefcase on a table, orders a whisky and tells the barman that he is 'bursting for a pee'. The landlord tells him to go through a doorway and turn left, which the desperate man does, undoing himself on the way. Thinking he is arriving at the toilet the man pulls out his 'apparatus', as it is referred to in the story, but finds himself standing on a platform in the public bar with his private parts on display. The barman sees him, is enraged, and throws the man out onto the street. Our hero returns to the saloon bar to retrieve his hat and briefcase, just as the barman is telling the landlord about what happened. After a shout of 'that's him!', the frustrated man, still not having had his pee, is thrown out onto the street again. Years later the man walks into a pub in Ipswich and sees the former City of London pub landlord behind the bar. 'Don't I know you?' the landlord asks.

A more cautionary tale is told in Paul Screeton's book *Mars Bars and Mushy Peas*, of the only child of a north London Cypriot family, who is left alone for the first time. Half an hour after his strict parents have left for their holiday in Limassol, the boy is smoking, drinking whisky and masturbating to hard-core porn while naked. If only he had waited longer; his parents soon came home, having forgotten their passports.

In 1978, a couple were caught out having sex in a small two-seater sports car somewhere in Regents Park. The near-naked man suffered a slipped disc, trapping the woman under '200 pounds of pain-racked, immobile man,' said a Dr Brian Richards. In her desperation to be free, the woman began honking the car horn with her foot. A crowd gathered, including women volunteer workers serving tea, while the fire brigade cut away the frame of the car. After the woman is finally helped out of the car and given a coat, she is distraught and asks, 'How am I going to explain to my husband what happened to his car?'

The Tumour in the Whale was published the same year (1978) and carried a similar story. The car was stuck for at least an hour at the end of someone's driveway before the homeowner went to investigate. The woman is more blasé after the rescue workers apologise for having to cut the top of her husband's car away. 'That's all right,' she says. 'It's not my husband.'

In the world of urban legends, getting a penis out in the wrong place can be lethal: I am sure most have heard the story of the man who accidently urinated on the electric rail of the London Underground and was killed by the electric current jumping back up at him. The man is usually drunk, and it is late at night so he thinks he can get away with his public urinating. Sometimes he thinks he is polluting a river, other times he is just so drunk he does not care. There is even a news story from the *Daily Mail* and *Evening Standard* newspapers on 22 July 2008 of an unnamed 41-year-old Polish tourist who died whilst urinating on the live rail at Vauxhall rail station.

Many doubt that you could electrocute yourself by weeing on an electric rail. In 2003, the American television programme *Mythbusters* tested the myth by constructing an anatomically correct man full of yellow liquid. The urine flow was compared to one of the male presenter's actual flow filmed on a high-speed camera. With the mannequin's flow all present and correct, it was released over a live rail. It became apparent that urine does not come out in a continuous stream, but quickly breaks into droplets on the way down, making it, the programme makers said, difficult if not impossible for the current to conduct back up to the penis and hands. Online discussion forums and comments are a useful place to pick up people talking about such ephemeral things as this. Online it was presumed that the initial shock would cause the man to jump, removing the flow from the rail. The voltage of an electric fence or rail line would not kill instantly, unlike in one tragic example in Monsanto of a man urinating on a downed power cable lying unseen in a ditch.

Whilst investigating the possibility, Chicago's The Straight Dope website found that in two cases in America of death by supposed 'electric wee' the victims had both made physical contact with the rail whilst urinating. So while the coroner's report could correctly state that the two people – an adult man and a 14-year-old boy – had died while urinating on an electric rail, it was the physical contact with the live rail during or afterwards that had killed them. It is possible that this is what happened at Vauxhall. The man died around 5.20 p.m. on 12 July, when it was light and there were plenty of witnesses. This is not the late-night lethal release of legend. It was reported in the *Metro* on 22 July 2008 that the man had gone onto the rail line to relieve himself, so it is possible that he physically touched the live rail while down there, as his body was found slumped over the track. I have not been able to check a coroner's report on the death and, in all honesty, do not wish to read it.

There are many things in this book that the reader should not try, most of them because they would frighten or harm other people, and despite the evidence gathered here that urinating on the electric rail of a train or tube line would not hurt or kill you, please do not try it yourself. No one will be impressed and it is a bit offensive. Wait until you get home, find a public loo or go and urinate in a pub toilet, so long as you have made sure you are undoing yourself in the toilet.

Either at noon, or in the afternoon when the sun shines through the club-shaped balustrades running the length of Westminster Bridge, the top section stretches to cause a row of sunny, phallus shapes to appear. At first I thought it was a digitally enhanced comment on the residents of the Houses of Parliament at the north end of the bridge. Sadly, I have not found the time to linger long on Westminster Bridge seeking illuminated penises, but one brave London member (sorry) of the Snopes message board did go to Westminster Bridge and, at 1.03 p.m., photo-graphed a raft of unfortunate shapes. This was after others had dismissed the image as 'completely unreal IMO [in my opin-ion]. The contrast between the light penii and the shadow looks wrong.' They were also wrong about the plural of penis.

The story that came with the genuine image was a joke about the Mayor of London, Boris Johnson, closing Westminster Bridge in the afternoons to avoid offending people with the luminous images. As pointed out on the Snopes board, whoever wrote the joke, taken seriously by readers outside the UK, did not know Boris Johnson and his inimitable wit. The website Liveleak attributed the appearance of the penises to the 2007 refurbishment of Westminster Bridge, when the balustrades were installed without thought to how their outlines may look in the long afternoon light.

So far the shape made by the balustrades of Westminster Bridge has only been attributed to perverts though, I am sure someone at some time will put a hidden-insult-style story to this trick of the light. The location near the Houses of Parliament is just too good not to. Let's wait and see …

LEGENDS OF ROCK

I'm in the kitchen with the tombstone blues.

✦

Bob Dylan, 'Tombstone Blues'

✦ 'It's taken you so long to ✦ find out you were wrong'

Hopefully everyone now knows that the late actor and quiz-show host of *Blockbusters*, Bob Holness, did not play the saxophone on Jerry Rafferty's hit song 'Baker Street'. The myth was invented by the author and radio presenter Stuart Maconie for the 'Believe It or Not' column of music paper the *NME* (the *New Musical Express*). Another version of the legends origin is that LBC DJ Tommy Boyd claims to have run a 'true or false' question on a quiz about the 'neat and tidy' Bob being able to turn out a raunchy sax break. Things become more confusing when we hear that the actual saxophonist on 'Baker Street', Raphael Ravenscroft, claims to have told a foreign journalist that Bob had played on the song when asked if it was he who had performed it for the twentieth or thirtieth time. Bob himself was said to have encouraged the myth; on one occasion on *Blockbusters* a question came up about the song 'Baker Street' and Bob winked into the camera and complimented the sax solo. He would also claim to be the guitarist on the Derek and the Dominos song 'Layla', and that he was the person responsible for making Elvis laugh on the notorious live version of 'Are You Lonesome Tonight?' The myth of Bob Holness on 'Baker Street' has begat myths of its own.

✧ 'Why go to learn the words of fools?' ✧

Another song myth that has not popped its head too high up into mainstream culture yet is the location of Itchycoo Park from The Small Faces' song of the same name. The first time I had a location pointed out to me, I was getting a lift from a work colleague called TBJ, who told me that Itchycoo Park was Altab Ali Park in Whitechapel, previously St Mary's Park and the former site of St Mary's Church. TBJ was a bit of a character, and at work he would tell stories of the characters at his local pub or gym, such as Jimmy Two Times, who was actually a gangster from the film *Goodfellas*.

I read Altab Ali Park's link to the song again in the 14 September 2012 e-newsletter from the indie music magazine *Artrocker*, where Tom Artrocker recounts:

> I spent a pleasant couple of hours in Whitechapel yesterday. The sun shone as the traffic roared towards the coast, I was there with my team to photograph and video Toy. We took photos in the middle of the traffic's roar, down a dark alley and, traditionalists that we are, against a brick wall. Then we headed a few yards to Altab

Ali Park. At which point I pointed out that prior to its re-naming, in honour of a young Bangladeshi murdered by several youths, this was the site of Itchycoo Park, as glorified by The Small Faces.

Small Faces member Ronnie Lane claimed that Little Ilford Park is Itchycoo Park. Tony Calder stated that the park story was invented by himself and the band to get around a BBC ban on the song and its possible drug references. Itchycoo Park was the name of a piece of wasteground in the East End that the band played on as children.

Valentines Park, West Ham and Wanstead Flats have all also been named as possible Itchycoo Park locations, although there is also the possibility that the song was inspired by a pamphlet about Oxford and has nothing to do with east London. Itchycoo Park is a pop music Atlantis or Camelot: it has many locations, some in London.

The name may have migrated from another nearby location: in his 1980 book *Rothschild Buildings: Life in an East End Tenement Block 1887–1920*, Jerry White describes 'Itchy Park' being Christ Church Gardens. This is the small ground beside Christ Church on Commercial Street, not too far from Altab Ali Park.

According to White's book, the park got its name from the children scratching themselves, like good East End urchins, against the railings of the park while using it as a playground. Tom Artrocker's origin for Itchy Park is even less kind, being from the fleas on the homeless people who used the park in the past and up to the present. The lyrics to 'Itchycoo Park' don't completely match either location; the dreaming spires could be the imposing steeple of Nicholas Hawksmoor's Christ Church, but there is no duck pond, and so no ducks to feed a bun to. We should not get too hung up on treating song lyrics as literal descriptions, however. If song writers are seeking to mirror reality in a lyric it would still be the first thing jettisoned for a pleasing rhyme or suitable mood.

✧ Liverpool Sunset ✧

Some stories become facts not by being true but by being short, sharp, easily communicable pieces of information. Ray Davies was a chronicler and satiriser of Sixties Britain and The Kinks' song 'Waterloo Sunset' was a description of swinging London, with its characters Terry and Julie meeting at Waterloo station every Friday night based upon the handsome icons of the era Julie Christie and Terence Stamp. Everyone knows that Ray Davies watched from his window as they crossed the river for untold adventures. You know it, I know it, Terence Stamp knew it when interviewed about his retrospective at the nearby British Film Institute in May 2013.

Facts are tricky things and not always based on any actual real occurrence, particularly when the reality of the fact comes from the often volatile mind of a writer or musician. 'Waterloo Sunset', the song stained with the tears of countless Londoners, a group not often given over to sentimentality, started life as a hymn to Mersey-beat called 'Liverpool Sunset'. The *Liverpool Echo* cheerfully quoted Ray Davies in its 14 May 2010 issue as saying 'Liverpool is my favourite city, and the song was originally called Liverpool Sunset,' going on to proclaim 'London was home, I'd grown up there, but I like to think I could be an adopted Scouser. My heart is definitely there.' It should be noted that Davies was about to play the Liverpool Philharmonic Hall when he gave the interview.

So Terry and Julie may have had very different accents? Probably not as, according to a 'Behind the Song' column in the *Independent* dated 9 March 1998, once the change was made from Liverpool to Waterloo, Davies could incorporate the scene of countless people flowing out of Waterloo underground like another dirty old river. The couple at the station were not Terence Stamp and Julie Christie, but Davies' young nephew Terry. Davies' brother-in-law had just emigrated to Australia and he imagined Arthur's young son grown-up, back in London and meeting his girlfriend. The *Independent* article speculated that Julie symbolised England, so may have been based on Julie Christie alone.

Is any of this true? Following the workings of a creative imagination is like trying to jog across a continuous landslide of ideas, images, thoughts and feelings, even long after the creative piece is complete. We will probably never know. If you do meet Terence Stamp however, it may be best not to mention that the Terry in 'Waterloo Sunset' is not him, but Davies' nephew, all grown up and living in a fictional future London. When asked about it by the *Evening Standard* in an interview about his retrospective, published 2 May 2013, Stamp growled:

> My brother Chris [ex-manger of The Who] … told me in the Seventies that when Ray Davies wrote 'Waterloo Sunset' he was thinking of me and Julie Christie. But apparently Ray denies it now. Well, if he says it's not true I don't care. I've believed it all these years …

✦ 'What's behind the green door?' ✦

A London urban legend, nipped as it was budding, attempted to link an esoteric London location to the rock-and-roll track 'Green Door'. The song is a plea from a desperate man trying to get through a green door and into a midnight party full of laughter and hot piano playing. The protagonist in the song never makes it in; when he tells the unknown revellers that 'Joe' had sent him, they merely laugh at him.

First performed by Jim Lowe and reaching No.1 in the charts in America, 'Green Door' got to No. 2 and No. 8 in the UK. A version by Frankie Vaughn reached No.2, another by Glen Mason reached No. 24 and in 1981 Shakin' Stevens got 'Green Door' to No. 1 for four weeks.

In the Friday, 8 September 2006 'Culture' section of the *Guardian* Brian Boyd attempted to put the lyrics into a surprising context. The green door of the song was in London, on Bramerton Street off the Kings Road in Chelsea. It was the door to The Gateway, a private lesbian bar or club. The bar was a location for the film *The Killing of Sister George*, the story of a lesbian love triangle. The story of 'Green Door' is of a man trying to get into a gay women-only bar. When he says 'Joe sent me', he is referring to Joe Meek, the gay British pioneering popstar, which only goes down as a joke with the club's regulars. In his article, Boyd was attempting to put 'Green Door' with other gay pop songs featured in the compilation album *From The Closet To The Charts*, though the full title of the album, compiled by John Savage, is *Queer Noises 61–78: From The Closet To The Charts*. 'Green Door' was first a hit in 1956. It is not as popular as 'Waterloo Sunset' or 'Itchycoo Park' and the explanation of their origins, but Boyd's theory did make it far enough to make it into Stephanie Theobald's top five lesbian songs list in the *Guardian* on 6 March 2007, but this mention comes with a correction and clarification on the website.

The lyrics of 'Green Door' were written by Marvin Moore, with music by Bob Davie and was composed in a four-room apartment they shared in Greenwich Village in New York. As a graduate of the Texas Christian University School of Journalism, it seems Moore would be unfamiliar with the goings-on of 1950s lesbian London, a decade when the majority of Londoners would be unfamiliar with the concept of a 'lesbian London'.

There are more convincing explanations of the meaning of 'Green Door': that the song's original singer, Jim Lowe, was singing about a bar with a green door called The Shack when he went to the University of Missouri, or that it is based on the 1940 novel *Behind the Green Door*, although whatever is happening behind the door, set in as ski-resort, does not resemble the fun in the song.

Perhaps the most satisfying explanation is that 'Green Door' is a response or shout-back to the song 'Hernando's Hideaway' from the musical *The Pajama Game*, which describes a secretive nightclub for a 'glass of wine and a fast embrace', and where the password to get in is 'Joe sent us'. The song was a hit the year before 'Green Door'.

✧ Metal Box ✧

Further off the mainstream radar is the discombobulating electronic music of Richard James, the Aphex Twin. His music can jump from serene to harsh to nausea-inducing. It is a fitting tribute to this that in the early 2000s the large stainless steel box in the centre of the Elephant and Castle roundabout was said to be his home. The box is, in fact, the Michael Faraday Memorial, dedicated to the scientist who was born nearby in Newington Butts. The monument itself contains an electrical substation for the Bakerloo and Northern tube lines and is not a house. The Aphex Twin lived nearby in the slightly more conventional venue of a converted bank.

✧ Bob Dylan's Crouch End Road Trip ✧

Researching things is great, not only because you find out things you want to know, but that you always happen upon strange and probably apocryphal facts you never knew you needed to look into. A story dated 15 August 1993 in the *Independent* newspaper tells me that Crouch End once had more curry houses than all of Austria. This does sound possible, although twenty years on and TripAdvisor is listing thirty-one Indian restaurants in Vienna alone.

I stumbled on this while reading up on the connection between megalithic American folk-rocker Bob Dylan and his visits to Crouch End. Apparently he viewed a house there back in 1993 and became a regular at the Shamrat of India curry house. 'I recognised him from the telly,' said the owner at the time, 'but I'm more of a Beatles fan myself.' Bob wasn't getting a lot of love in Crouch End back then – the owner of the local guitar shop said that 'he used to be good, but he's rubbish now.'

According to urban legend a further indignity for Dylan may have happened around the same time. The real untrue story of Bob Dylan in Crouch End begins with his friendship with Dave Stewart of the Eurythmics, who once owned a recording studio called the Crypt, on 145 Crouch Hill. Stewart invited Dylan round, saying that the next time he was in Crouch End he should visit the studio. Dylan was seemingly so keen that he gave the studio's address at the airport so he could go straight there. Unfortunately the taxi driver dropped Dylan off, not at Dave Stewart's grand recording studio in an old church, but on nearby Crouch End Hill, where No. 145 was a house. Dylan knocked on the door, asked for Dave and to compound his series of unfortunate events a Dave did live at the house, but was out at the time. Dave's wife said that he would be back soon, so would the mumbling American gentleman like to come in and wait for him? And would he like a cup of tea? Dave the plumber later arrived home and asked his wife if there were any messages for him. She said, 'No, but Bob Dylan's in the living room having a cup of tea.'

Writer Emma Hartley investigated the story for her 'Emma Hartley's Glamour Cave' folk music blog in a post dated, of course, 1 April 2013. She rang the Crypt studio and was told by an Anthony Lerner that he had 'heard it from the man who was Dave Stewart's chief sound engineer at that time'. Emma went out to Crouch End to knock on the door of the house on Crouch End Hill. It was while walking up the hill that she discovered that there is no No. 145. Perhaps the taxi driver was even more cloth-eared than we thought and took Dylan to

No. 45 Crouch End Hill, which was, at least in the 1891 census, a residential property. Or perhaps the whole story is made up.

Consoling herself with a drink at Banner's Restaurant, No. 21 Park Road, Crouch End, she spotted a mural on the side of the building showing Bob Dylan asking, 'Don't you know who I am?' Inside, Emma was shown a brass plaque declaring that 'Bob Dylan sat at this table, August 1993'. Apparently, after his ill-fated trip to a possibly non-existent house on Crouch End Hill, Dylan went to console himself with a drink. At the time, however, Banner's alcohol licence did not allow people to have a drink without food, so Bob Dylan was turned down. He asked them 'Do you know who I am?' just so the restaurant staff were sure of who they were denying booze. The response is not recorded, but it seems like Bob Dylan just can't get a break in Crouch End.

NEW LEGENDS
AS OLD

They were not history, but legends ...

✦

Steve Roud, London Lore

✧ The Deptford Jolly Roger ✧

Tucked down a street that's off another street that comes off
Creek Road in Deptford is St Nicholas Church. The churchyard is dense and old, and Elizabethan playwright Christopher
Marlow is buried somewhere in its grounds. On the gateposts
leading into the churchyard is another of the church's famous
features: two large decaying, yet still grinning, stone skulls crossed
with bones underneath. This striking feature has acquired a
legend to suit its visual impact, because these skulls and crossbones are the inspiration for the pirate flag, the Jolly Roger.

Deptford's maritime history is mostly obliterated, save a couple of warehouses and watergates by the river, but it was once the 'King's Yard', having been founded by Henry VIII, remaining a naval and shipping hub until after the Napoleonic Wars. Captain James Cook's ship the HMS *Resolution* set off from and was refitted at the dockyard, and Sir Francis Drake was knighted by Elizabeth I aboard the *Golden Hind* at Deptford. By the 1840s ships had become larger, and the shallow, narrow bed of the river made getting to Deptford difficult, closing the area to major shipping.

With over 300 years of naval history, Deptford must have had its fair share of pirates, or would-be pirates, passing St Nicholas Church on their way to their ship, the tavern or even to their execution. Many of them who looked up were inspired by these blood-curdling sculptures enough to incorporate their likeness into their flag and spread the terror of it across the seas.

London bloggers, ever on the lookout for an eye-opening and quirky fact, love the story. An undated 'Summer Strolls' walk around Deptford published by *Time Out* mentions the legend; even the website of St Nicholas and St Luke's churches repeats the story, although keeps its factual possibility at fingertips' length. The site describes the skull and crossbones flag as a means for British privateer sailors ('freelance' sailors who were paid on commission, working for the British Navy, fighting against the French, Spanish and Dutch ships for the control of the world's trade routes) to hide their nationality by flying the Jolly Roger rather than the English or Union Flag. The Information Britain website even names Henry Morgan, a former British admiral turned privateer who must have been familiar with Deptford, as the St Nicholas parishioner who first got the idea.

The difference between a privateer and a pirate is who benefits from the loot you steal. Henry Morgan was privateering for England and would have flown the English flag as he raided and looted innocent (or enemy) ships.

Historically, the Jolly Roger was not a ubiquitous symbol of piracy and was not adopted as a universal symbol of the pirate's outlaw status. Pirate flags were more in keeping with naval rules of engagement than the attitude of criminals. When one ship attacked another, a red flag was flown to indicate that they were in conflict. If the attacking ship was victorious, it would take the ship and its cargo and take the surviving crew prisoner, or 'give quarter'. To fly a black flag meant to give no quarter: the attacking ship would take no prisoners, so to avoid a slaughter the defending ship had best surrender without a fight. Pirates favoured the black flag, as often this is what would happen; even when outnumbered, enemy ships would surrender to avoid a massacre.

Over time, pirates began to decorate their black flags with personal symbolism in a seventeenth- and eighteenth-century example of 'pimping' something up: Thomas Tew's black flag showed an arm holding a dagger; Edward Teach, the infamous Blackbeard, flew a black flag featuring a skeleton stabbing a heart with an arrow; Bartholomew Roberts, Black Bart, had himself on his flag, holding one side of an hourglass with Death holding the other side. (This was followed by an even more flamboyant flag of himself holding a dagger and a flaming sword, with each foot on a skull). Calico Jack, John Rackam, flew a skull crossed with swords underneath while Henry Every flew a skull in profile with crossed bones beneath; not quite the symbol on the Deptford church. Edward English, born in Ireland, did fly the skull and crossbones, but there are few records of his early life and it is not known whether he visited Deptford.

The skull and crossbones itself is an old symbol that had already graced Spanish graveyards by the time St Nicholas was built. The earliest mention of pirates raising the skull and crossbones comes from a logbook entry dated 6 December 1687. It reads: 'And we put down our white flag, and raised a red flag with a Skull head on it and two crossed bones (all in white and in the middle of the flag), and then we marched on.' There may be a possibility that a pirate, when designing his own flag, thought of St Nicholas in Deptford and copied the design. That pirate did not do it so well, though. As the church's website points out, the skulls wear a laurel-wreath on their heads, probably to signify the victory over death over transient flesh. This wreath has not made it on to any pirate flags. It is still a story loved in Deptford, though. A local pub, the Bird's Nest, has even nicknamed itself the 'pirate pub' due to the Jolly Roger legend.

✧ The London Stone ✧

History can be hidden in plain sight in the dustiest and busiest locations. Opposite Cannon Street station, set behind a metal grid in front of a branch of WHSmith sits the London Stone. The stone was the centre of a story in 2012 that named it as essential to the survival of London itself. It had been in its approximate location for a millennia or two, but the redevelopment of Cannon Street meant that property company Minerva wanted to move the stone, so that they could demolish the 1960s office block it occupies. The plan was to place it in the corner of its gleaming new Walbrook building on the corner of Cannon Street and Walbook. 'The new dedicated setting will enhance the significance of the asset,' Minerva wrote in 2011, 'and better reveal its significance for current and future generations.' Minerva did not, however, count on newspapers reporting the story with fears that moving the stone would be disaster to London. The *Evening Standard*, along with other papers, discovered an ancient saying that read: 'So long as the Stone of Brutus is safe, so long will London flourish.'

The London Stone is oolitic limestone and no one knows why it is there or what its original purpose was. It may have been part of a monument in front of the palace of a provincial Roman governor, which lay where Cannon Street is now. It may be a Saxon milestone of some sort: its original location is also the centre of Saxon London when it was re-established by King Alfred in AD 886. The stone has had its name since the twelfth century; an address recorded in a document dated between 1098 and 1108 is 'Eadwaker aet lundene stane'. In his 1598 *Survey of London*, Stow writes of 'a great stone called London Stone, fixed in the ground very deep, fastened with iron bars.' It is thought that it was damaged in the Great Fire of London in 1666, which possibly reduced it to something near its current size; the stone was placed by the door of the rebuilt St Swithin's Church.

Things start to get strange for the London Stone, as far as we know, from Jack Cade's 1450 rebellion. Cade, invading the City of London, struck the London Stone and declared himself the mayor of London. As John Clark, former Senior Curator (Medieval) at the Museum of London points out, much of our knowledge of this event comes from Shakespeare's dramatic interpretation in *Henry VI Part 2*. Clark points out that there is no historical precedent for the Lord Mayor having to strike the London Stone, and contemporary chronicles were 'at a loss as to its significance'. In the 1720 update to Stow's *Survey of London,* John Strype got druids involved for the first time, suggesting that the stone was 'an Object, or Monument, of Heathen Worship'. London poet and mystic William Blake ran with the idea, suggesting that it was a Druid altar stone. Thomas Pennant, in his *Some Account of London*, suggested that the London Stone could have 'formed part of a druidical circle'. The idea that the stone somehow protected London was first considered in Pennant's *Account*:

> At all times it has been preserved with great care, placed deep
> in the ground, and strongly fastened with bars of iron. It seems
> preserved, like the palladium of the city.

This refers to the statue of Pallas Athene that protected the city of Troy. This all fitted very well into the legend first concocted by twelfth-century writer Geoffrey of Monmouth in his *History of the Kings of Britain* that Brutus of Troy brought the Brutus Stone to Britain after his city's destruction, and ancient kings would swear oaths over it. After all, didn't Jack Cade strike the stone and declare himself ruler of London? Perhaps the London Stone is the stone of Brutus? There is already a Brutus Stone in Totnes where the refugee Trojan landed, but that probably doesn't matter. The first to suggest that the London Stone is the stone of Brutus seems to be Welsh supremacist and language advocate Revd Richard Williams Morgan under his nom de plume Môr Meirion. In 1892, in an article in 'Notes and Queries', a pre-internet user-generated content publication where questions were asked and answered by public correspondence, Morgan is the first to 'discover' the ancient saying 'so long as the Stone of Brutus is safe, so long will London flourish'. In his 1857 book *The British Kymry, Or Britons of Cambria*, Morgan suggested that the London Stone is the palladium of Troy, possibly dragged under the wooden horse as the city burned. The *Newburgh Telegraph* of 18 December 1909 described the stone as a 'relic of Homer's days'.

In the twentieth and twenty-first centuries the London Stone was incorporated into a number of ley-lines (lines that can be drawn through a number of sacred sites to decipher arcane truths about the sacred landscape). By 2002 the London Stone was linked to Elizabethan occultist John Dee, in a claim that he believed it had magical powers. It was even given another legendary secret identity as the stone from which King Arthur drew Excalibur. These stories came out suspiciously near to London's bid for the 2012 Olympics.

There is little danger in moving the London Stone: in fact, it was moved from the centre of Cannon Street in 1720 when it became a traffic hazard. It was incorporated into the post-Great Fire St Swithin's Church. As a part of the church furniture, it moved around a little until it ended up in the corner of the church. Come 1884, when the District Line was being constructed, the London Stone was kept where it was, but the earth beneath it was removed. St Swithin's was gutted by Second World War bombing and the stone was moved to its current location in 1961, when the offices at 111 Cannon Street were built. At the time of writing, part of the new Cannon Street gleams under the spring sun while older buildings are being closed down in anticipation of demolition. The London Stone still sits in its tatty 1960s site, accompanied by a huge sign advertising cheap office space.

✧ The Ravens in the Tower ✧

One of London's most famous pieces of folklore is of the ravens of the Tower of London. Everyone knows, or knows of, the saying 'If the Tower of London ravens are lost or fly away, the Crown will fall and Britain with it.' This is why the wings of the ravens are clipped so they do not fly away. Why would the ravens even be in a book full of upstart urban legends? Could the London Stone legend be a corruption of this famous piece of tradition?

One story of how the ravens gained their power over our nation comes via the first astronomer royal, John Flamstead. As is the way with these things, there are two versions of the story. The first has Flamstead and King Charles II gazing through telescopes in Greenwich when their view is obscured by ravens. They were frustrating Flamstead by either flying in front of the telescopes or defecating on the lens. Charles II said that the ravens must go, but Flamstead told the monarch that it is unlucky to kill a raven and that 'if the ravens left the Tower, the White Tower [the oldest part of the Tower of London] would collapse and a great disaster would befall the Kingdom'. In other versions of the tale it is an obscure soothsayer who warns the king after Flamstead complains about the ravens.

However, when Dr Parnell, official Tower of London historian, went through records of the Tower of London's menagerie he found records of hawks, lions, leopards, monkeys and a polar bear, but no mention of a raven. Dr Parnell along with American writer Boria Sax, who was also interested in the Tower's raven-lore, went through as much literature as possible and found the earliest mention of ravens at the Tower in a supplement called *The Pictorial World* on the Tower of London from 1883.

Where the legend itself comes from is another story, the earliest written version found only dates as far back as 1955, although the legend was recorded earlier. Natsume Soseki was a Japanese writer sent to study in London in 1900. He visited the Tower and wrote an account that Boria Sax describes as 'phantasmagoric'. Soseki entered the Tower like it was a gothic nightmare, and 'met' the ghosts of Guy Fawkes, Walter Raleigh and Lady Jane Grey. The ghost of Lady Jane tells a child, who can only see three ravens, that there are always five. Soseki writes the following on his encounter with a raven up-close and his thoughts on the Tower's executions: 'Hunching its wings, its black beak protruding, it stares at people. I feel as if the rancour of a hundred years of blood have congealed and taken the form of a bird so as to guard this unhappy place for ever.'

Returning to his lodgings, Soseki is told by his landlord: 'They're sacred ravens. They've been keeping them there since ancient times, and, even if they become one short, they immediately make up the numbers again. There are always five ravens there.'

Soseki's account was not translated into English until much later, but it is possible he picked up a folk-belief gathering around the idea of the ravens. Sax compares the impressionistic way Soseki writes to James Joyce's novel *Ulysses*, representing the world of London as Joyce represents Dublin, but threading it with fiction. No one at present can ascertain where one ends and the other takes over.

Could the raven myth have been created earlier? It may not be much of a surprise that Dr Parnell did not find ravens in the Tower's menagerie because ravens have long been indigenous to London. To record them at the Tower would be the same as listing the pigeons at London Zoo. Another suggestion for the ravens' presence was that they were a joke gift to the Tower by the 3rd Earl of Dunraven. Dunraven was interested in Celtic raven myths (he had ravens incorporated into his family crest) and must have known the Welsh legends of the *Mabinogion*. One tells of the hero-giant Bran being fatally wounded in battle and having his head removed and taken to Gwynfryn, a white hill in London with his head placed looking toward France so he could always keep Britain safe. Many think the white hill is the hill the White Tower is built on. Then myth-makers will nod as they tell you the word Bran, in Welsh, means 'crow', which is almost like a raven.

The ritual of the raven numbers is embedded now, whatever its origin. Interviewed for the *Fortean Times* issue 206, Yeoman Ravenmaster Derek Coyle repeated the Charles II legend and that there must always be six ravens at the Tower by Charles' decree. It may be possible that wandering through early twentieth-century London, Soseki misheard the number as five instead of six. While Coyle does not mention the legend directly, he does say that he keeps twelve birds at other locations to be sent for if numbers at the Tower drop too low. The cynical suspect that the story of the ravens was an extra fable created for tourists that Londoners took to their hearts too. The truth is that there were no ravens in the Tower of London by the end of the Second World War, as some ravens had died in bombing raids and others had pined away or died of shock. By the time the Tower was reopened in 1946, a new set had been found. Their wings are clipped to stop them leaving, not because the Tower may fall if they do, but because it is very difficult to stop ravens from flying away.

◇ The Lions in the Tower ◇

The ravens in the Tower urban legends may have been inspired by the London Stone story, but also by an earlier animal fable of the Tower. London Zoo started life as the Royal Menagerie at the Tower of London, with the lions being the most popular. John Ashton, writing in his 1883 *Social Life in the Reign of Queen Anne*, reports that seeing the lions at the Tower was the first thing all those new to London did, and that when three of the four lions died in 1903, it was thought to be a 'dire portent'. The lives of the lions of the Tower were inextricably linked to the lives of the sovereign. In 1603, when one of the lions died just before the death of Queen Elizabeth I, it was seen as portentous. Joseph Addison went to the Tower just after the unsuccessful Jacobite rising of 1715, with a friend sympathetic to the Jacobite cause. The plan was to install James II's son on the throne. The friend asked if any of the lions had fallen ill after the would-be king was defeated at Perth and fled, and was told the lions were in the best of health. Addison wrote: 'I found he was extremely startled, for he had learned from his cradle that the Lions in the Tower were the best judges of the title of our British Kings, and always sympathise with our sovereigns.'

In earlier, less certain centuries, the fate of the nation and its people depended far more greatly on the monarch than now. It may be possible to think that the link between the lions' lives to that of the king transferred itself, once the lions left in 1835, to concerns about the nation connected to the ravens.

Once the lions had moved out of the Tower, they still managed to be an attraction there. Once a year, tickets would go out to people inviting them to the Tower to witness the washing of the lions. The invites were sent out in error in 1860, long after the lions had left the Tower, and the day of the 'annual ceremony' became 1 April. The meeting place was the fictional 'White Gate' to the Tower, and *The Chambers Book of Days* reported that on the day, cabs 'rattled about Tower Hill all that Sunday morning, vainly endeavouring to discover the White Gate'.

LEGENDARY LANDMARKS

··

*London is a wide place and a long, but rumour
has a wider scope and a longer tongue.*

✦

J. Fisher Murray, Physiology of London Life

··

WILLIAM KENT, IN his 1951 book *Walks in London*, recounts a story related to one of London's top tourist spots, St Paul's Cathedral. A boy from Snowdon was at a job interview at local textile manufacturers Hitchcock, Williams & Co., who were founded in St Paul's churchyard. The interviewer asked him if he had ever climbed to the top of the mountain. The boy said he had not, and was told there was 'no vacancy for one who was so unenterprising'. The next day, the boy returned and told his interviewer that he had just climbed up to the ball of St Paul's Cathedral. He asked the man, who worked for years in the shadow of St Paul's dome, whether he had ever done so, and the interviewer had to admit that he had not. The boy's point was taken; he was employed and was 'proved a most profitable servant'.

A nice story about how Londoners, like most people, often don't visit the wonders on their doorstep. Londoners I've known almost take pride in some of the London landmarks they have not visited, although these are often seen as lowbrow tourist places such as Madame Tussauds, the Trocadero and Covent Garden Market. They would be less likely to admit to never going to the Victoria & Albert museum or the Globe. Like the St Paul's story, there is probably a busy life involved too – Londoners live and work in London, and sometimes something in your immediate locale just doesn't seem like a priority. Stories that tell of success from unconventional ingenuity in job interviews always touches anyone who has had to undergo the rigours of interviewing for a position. This is a successful story. So successful, in fact, that it's had an American remake.

Kent goes on to repeat another story which appeared in *The Times* on 19 August 1950. It told of a Londoner visiting New York for the first time, who was early for meeting a friend. He nervously took the express elevator to the top of the skyscraper his appointment was in and was rewarded with an amazing vista of the city from the roof. Full of admiration, the Londoner told his friend about the view but the friend, a busy 'New Yorker born and bred', smiled superciliously and snapped that he didn't have the time 'for such rubber-necking'.

The Londoner didn't back down and told his friend that he should be ashamed of not taking advantage of the fine things on his doorstep. The New Yorker, with a broader smile, asked his Londoner pal how the view was from the top of St Paul's. It was the Londoner's turn to smile, the story says, as he had passed the cathedral every day on the way to work and had never gone beyond the Whispering Gallery.

Kent doesn't spot this as an urban legend; the term and concept was not around when Kent was writing *Walks in London*.

He does point out that his first story of the Snowdonian inter-viewee had been published, by him, some time before the New York version appeared. Perhaps other versions existed before the Snowdonian story that tells of the busy lives of Londoners and the things they do not get to do.

◇ Neil? Kneel! ◇

On 1 September 1983, *Los Angeles Times* columnist Jack Smith recounted a story of American tourists visiting the Houses of Parliament on a holiday in London. The story goes that they encountered Sir Quentin Hogg, Lord Hailsham, the Keeper of the Woolsack, 'resplendent in the gold and scarlet robes of his office topped by a ceremonial wig'. The pomp of the Houses of Parliament is intimidating to Londoners, so the effect on a corri-dor of American tourists by this visitation must have been great. Then Lord Hailsham sees, beyond the tourists, his friend the Hon. Neil Matten MP. He shouts his friend's name: 'Neil! Neil!'

The crowd of tourists fall into embarrassed silence and then fall to their knees.

While this story very clearly illustrates American confusion and awkwardness when faced with British parliamentary pomp, it does not illustrate life in the Palace of Westminster. There is no Keeper of the Woolsack in UK Parliament; Sir Quintin Hogg was Lord Chancellor, who sits on the woolsack in the House of Lords and is custodian of the Great Seal, a symbol of the sovereign's approval of state documents. The Lord Chancellor is responsible for the Great Seal unless a Keeper of the Great Seal is appointed. Parliamentary process can baffle anyone beyond its sphere, so there is no shame in confusing the details, but it does put doubt on the story.

There has also never been a Neil Matten in the House of Commons. Neil Marten was the Conservative MP for Banbury between 1959 and 1983. According to Andrew Roth's

The MPs' Chart, Marten was a 'pro-commonwealth, anti-EEC … witty, sharp, tense, neat, balding, wartime agent'. Hogg and Marten were Conservatives together and certainly knew each other. The story, with its confused titles and 'scrawled on the back of a beer mat' – misspelling both men's names – has the air of a story told verbally, hastily written down and then repeated without checking any details.

In his *Los Angeles Times* column, Jack Smith was using this story as a way of tracing an American urban legend. A tale titled 'The Elevator Incident' by Jan Harold Brunvand in *The Choking Doberman and Other 'New' Urban Legends*, describes a small group of women getting into an elevator in New York. A man gets into the elevator with them and makes the command to 'sit'. The women sit, causing the man to apologise, as he was talking to the dog. At this point the man is revealed to be a celebrity who treats the women to dinner.

✧ The Waters of Senate House ✧

The imposing University College of London building Senate House keeps going below ground level. Standing at its base, in several places, is a drop showing lower levels of the building created to bring natural light into the basement levels. This gully has water gushing out of it in numerous places, giving it the name of 'the moat'. Researching Senate House folklore for her project 'The Ghosts of Senate House', the artist Sarah Sparks recorded stories of a spring, lake or pond beneath the building. John Stone, the Building Services Technical Officer, took her into a lower basement to show the source of the water.

> Water is flowing through a fissure in the wall and collecting on the floor. The duck boards dotted along the tunnel serve as stepping stones and were placed there when the building was first

constructed showing that the water was always present. A channel two inches by two inches has been carved into the stone floor to allow the water to flow into a sump pumping the water up to The Moat above.

She then goes on to speculate that:

Geologists, employed to investigate the water, suggest that a spring up to a mile away has been diverted by building work however, this does not account for the fact that the water has been present to a greater or lesser extent since the buildings construction. I speculate that this water may originate from one of the lost rivers of London, possibly the Fleet. John agrees that there may be some truth in this citing that recent excavations of North Block Green unearthed an old conduit.

The Fleet is a mile or two away from Senate House, slurping under Farringdon Road and Farringdon Street through the Fleet Sewer. Speaking to Sarah about the water some months later, she told me an investigation had found that the water was coming from a leaking water main and not some lost spring or river. However, by September 2013 the leak has yet to be found.

The water has been there since before Senate House. Charles Holden, the architect, reported that one of the few problems he had with the construction of the building was a large pocket of water in the building's foundations. It was decided it should be left, as pumping it out could destabilise surrounding buildings as the ground moved to fill the gap left by it. The joists are said to pass through the water and into the clay beneath.

Londoners love the idea of our lost rivers, so it may not be surprising that another one is being used as a way of drawing people into a building. In his book *London's Lost Rivers: A Walker's Guide*, Tom Bolton described the River Tyburn's appearance in the basement of Gray's Antique Market on Davies Mews off

South Molton Lane. The market owners moved into the building in 1977 and found the basement flooded. Claiming the water was the Tyburn, they channelled it into a twee model river with a small bridge and goldfish. The owners of the building take their attraction seriously, putting signs up instructing visitors to not touch the waters of this working river. Tom is not so sure, pointing out that while the Tyburn does flow under South Molton Lane, the river flows through a sewer so would not be fit to be channelled through a building. The water is possibly from groundwater springs that may have fed the Tyburn before it was buried and enclosed.

THE SUICIDAL
SCULPTOR

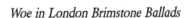

In London, starving workers dine
With old Duke Humphrey; as for wine,
'Twas made by Christ, in 'Auld Lang Syne'
But now he's turned teetotaler.

✦

Woe in London Brimstone Ballads

✧ Unknown Stone ✧

If we can be certain of one thing in London, it must be our
statues. To be set in stone suggests confidence and permanence,
and London's representations of its great and good must be a
solid link back to the best of our shared past. 'Dining with Duke
Humphrey' is a sweet but sad expression from sixteenth- and
seventeenth-century London which means, in short, to be too
poor to be able to afford dinner. The homeless and hungry lost

scholars would congregate by a memorial of the hospitable Duke Humphrey of Gloucester (1391–1447) in the grounds of St Paul's Cathedral.

This event becomes sadder still when one realises that the cenotaph at the centre of this crowd is not for 'Good Duke Humphrey' but Sir John Beauchamp. London's oldest outdoor indigenous statue (not counting anything ancient, lifted and shipped in from Egypt) is of King Alfred the Great, a bearded and caped figure who is believed to have once stood in the Palace of Westminster and who is now slumming it in Trinity Square in Southwark.

However, the 1910 book *Return of Outdoor Memorials in London* by the London County Council could not find any reference to who the statue might be, and lists it as Alfred with a question mark by it. The book notes: 'The Secretary of Trinity House states that the Corporation have endeavoured to ascertain the facts in connection with the origin of the statue, but without success.' Understandably, due to the blank drawn about its origins, the statue's status as London's oldest is uncertain too. King Alfred is thought to date back to the fourteenth century. The statute of Queen Elizabeth I that stands on the façade of St Dunstan-in-the-West can also claim to be the oldest, as it was erected during the Queen's reign, either in or around 1586. Nearby are the statues of London's mythical founder, King Lud and his son Tenvantius, who may have first been erected on the gates at Ludgate in 1586.

Another mystery memorial is the 'Eagle Pillar' that stands in Orme Square, just off Bayswater. No one can remember what the double pillar with an eagle on the top is there to represent. The theories are that it was erected by a grateful Mr Orme, who made a fortune selling gravel to Russia; that it is a French eagle in honour of Louis Napoleon's stay on the square, and/or that it commemorates the French Embassy, which once stood at No. 2 Orme Square. Or the eagle could in fact be a phoenix for a fire insurance company; the Geograph website notes that a 'nearby house has birds looking like phoenixes in its frontage'. The final guess in *Return of Outdoor Memorials of London* is a bit fed up with all the rest; it merely suggests that 'the column is not a memorial at all, but simply an ornament picked up in a builder's yard'.

✦ Suicidal Sculptors ✦

If we are uncertain about London's oldest stone statue, we're fairly certain that our oldest bronze statue, cast in 1633, is of King Charles I on horseback, which now stands at one end of the Mall by Trafalgar Square. The statue itself was cast just before the start of the Civil War in 1642, and on the outbreak of the war it was taken from its original spot on King Street, Covent Garden, and hidden in the crypt of the church of St Paul. During the interregnum, it was sold to a brazier named John Rivett, who was given orders to break it up. The canny Rivett broke the statue up by making and selling nutcrackers, thimbles and spoons made from the bronze of the dead king's statue. When the Restoration arrived, Rivett was able to provide the new Royalists with the fully intact statue that he had in storage.

This could be the urban legend about the statue of King Charles, but there is another attached which has proven to have far greater longevity and pedigree. In a letter dated 6 December 1725, Cesar de Saussure, from Lausanne, encountered the statue and recorded the story of the sculptor who had been 'almost beside himself with joy and pride' at his creation. However, on taking a closer look at the equestrian statue he realised the sculptor had forgotten to include the girths of the saddle (the strap or belt that goes around the horse that keeps saddle and rider on). The sculptor was so distraught to see his error set in bronze under the king's image that he hanged himself. 'This man was without doubt an Englishman' spat de Saussure, 'this trait depicts his energetic character.'

A community constable told Jeremy Harte of the Folklore Society that the reason the fourth plinth on Trafalgar Square is empty is because a huge equestrian sculpture was planned to be placed on it, and the sculptor was confident it would be his masterwork. The day was set for the unveiling, the sculpture waited under a huge sheet, dignitaries gathered and a band played for the ceremony. The sheet was removed and the crowd began to laugh because the sculptor had left the stirrups off his masterwork. The sculptor was so humiliated he ran down Northumberland Avenue and threw himself into the Thames.

This story has legs, six of them. It has also travelled over to the statue of the Duke of Wellington outside the Royal Exchange in the City. In a letter in the June 2002 issue of *FLS News*, John Spencer half-remembers having the statue's lack of stirrups pointed out to him by his grandfather and being told that the sculptor only realised his mistake when the king arrived to unveil the statue. Overcome with shame and embarrassment, the sculptor skulked off and shot himself. A year later, John was looking at the statue of George III in Windsor Great Park and overheard a middle-aged man explaining to a boy that the sculptor realised too late that the statue was stirrup-less and so committed suicide.

In reality, the sculptor of the Charles I statue was not an energetic Englishman, but a fellow Frenchman to de Saussure named Hubert Le Sueur. As well as the equestrian bronze, Le Sueur cast busts for England's royalty and aristocracy. Once the English Civil War began, his commissions naturally dried up and he moved back to France to work. He vanished into obscurity afterwards, long after the Charles I statue had been unveiled. The sculptor of the George III statue at Windsor Park portrayed him riding like a Roman, and the Romans did not use stirrups.

The fourth plinth in Trafalgar Square is not empty because of a shameful event involving stirrups. The original plan was for an equestrian statue of William IV to be placed there, but the plan was abandoned due to lack of funds. Another rumour about the plinth is that it is now reserved until after the death of Elizabeth II, so a statue of her can be placed there.

I have heard the legend told about the Maiwand Lion that stands in Forbury gardens in Reading, down the road from Windsor. The sculptor, George Blackall Simonds, is said to have killed himself on realising (after it had been completed) that the lion, one of the world's largest cast-iron statues, was incorrectly represented. Its stance is said to look more like a domestic cat walking than that of a lion.

Farther afield is the story of another enthusiastic English sculptor who threw himself into the Danube when he heard that the lions he had designed for the Chain Bridge in Budapest had been cast without tongues. These Hungarian lions are stone, not metal, and were certainly carved with tongues; it's just that they can only be seen from above.

✧ Backward Buildings ✧

The eighteenth-century Fort George, on the coast between Nairn and Inverness in Scotland, was apparently designed to be invisible from the sea, but when the architect rode out to view this on completion (why not before?) he could still see one small piece of the fort and so reached for a handy pistol nearby to shoot himself.

The most famous error of this type is the Kelvingrove Art Gallery and Museum in Glasgow, which is said to have been built the wrong way round with a modest entrance for the public at one end and two imposing turrets for the back entrance. It is said that when the architect discovered the error, he leapt to his death from the building. In truth, of course, the building had not been built backwards and the architect probably does not haunt his cursed building. Frank Crocker, however, is said to haunt the hotel he built on Aberdeen Place in NW8. It was built not the wrong way round but in the wrong place. Crocker believed that the terminus for the Great Central Railway would arrive at St John's Wood, and so he went about building the Crown pub and hotel on Aberdeen Place between 1898 and 1899, in anticipation of the masses. It was a fine building with a marble bar and fireplace and guest rooms with imitation Jacobean plaster. Adding another layer to the myth is the Shady Old Lady blog, which says the sly architect of the building managed to get his dig in by including a bust of the Emperor Caracalla in the pub, a Roman emperor known for his 'architectural excesses and his complete insanity'. Caracalla is remembered for his massacres and the exuberant public baths he is said to have commissioned in Rome. However, the London terminus for the line ended at Marylebone, not St John's Wood. And so, ruined financially with nothing to show except a grand hotel with no customers, Crocker jumped out of a high window and the pub's name changed from the Crown to Crockers Folly. The Doctor Johnson pub in Barkingside, east London, has the same story to explain its size: it was built to service the users of a new road in and out of London which never arrived.

As Antony Clayton points out in *The Folklore of London*, the Doctor Johnson pub is so large because it is an 'improved' public house to serve the growing housing estates on the edge of London. The Crown Hotel, aka 'Crockers Folly', was completed about the same time as Marylebone station, and so was not positioned on Aberdeen Place by mistake. While Frank Crocker died relatively early at the age of 41, his death was of natural causes.

The sculptor or architect's mistake, followed by suicide, is a story that must always be hanging in the air, waiting to attach itself to a large building or statue or when something is out of place or missing, like Charles I's saddle girth. The narrative is then inevitable: the grand project, some hubristic pride, the realisation of the error and then the shameful ending.

THE DEVILS
OF CORNHILL

THE BEST WAY to find the devils of Cornhill is to walk
north from London Bridge, up the west side of Gracechurch
Street, through the city of London toward Liverpool Street
station. Just before you get to the corner shared with Cornhill is
one side of St Peter upon Cornhill Church. Its white stone is caked
with a layer of grime and three tousle-haired cherubim, with
wings round their necks like ruffs, gazing aloof and detachedly
across the street. You then turn from Gracechurch Street into
Cornhill, glance up, and leering down at you is a red terracotta

demon with a dog-like body and a yowling, distended maw. It also has breasts, and a demonic face, its arms and chest are human. On the apex of the building crouches another larger demon, smirking to himself as he watches the passers-by on Cornhill. He looks as if he is preparing to launch himself onto an unsuspecting city worker or passing vicar below. It's a busy street, but I suspect few people feel comfortable loitering at this particular spot.

The story is of a nineteenth-century vicar at St Peter upon Cornhill who noticed that the planned new building on 54-55 Cornhill impinged on the church's land by 1ft. The vicar, or verger, disputed this and successfully stopped the building's construction. The builder, or architect, had to re-draw their plans and, as his revenge, he raised three devils (there's a smaller one beneath the top demon) onto the building overlooking the church and street to glare down on churchgoers and passers-by. In her own retelling of the story, the Shady Old Lady blog says that 'the devil closest to the street apparently bears more than a passing resemblance to the unlucky rector' as an extra twist. The oldest versions of the legend I have found date back to 1950, about fifty-three years after the building's construction. One, from 22 February of that year, is in Peter Jackson's compilation of *London Evening News* cartoons of London history and ephemera, titled *London is Stranger than Fiction*. It says: 'Crouching high up on an office building in Cornhill, stone devils glare down at the church of St Peter, below. They were put there by an architect who had just lost a dispute with the church authorities and erected them as a small token of his displeasure.'

William Kent's 1951 book, *Walks in London,* says: 'If we look across the road at this point we shall see high up on No. 54 a devil in stone. A legend says a builder had a feud with the Church and told them to go to the devil. A curse was laid upon him, but defiantly he erected this figure.'

In 1988, estate agents Baker Harris Saunders published details of 54-55 Cornhill when letting it, which included this urban legend as a piece of local colour. 'Legend has it that following a disagreement between the owner of the land and the adjacent church […] the owner sought retribution by adorning the building with a crouching devil and a chimera.' The truth of the legend is fudged and the leaflet gets the church wrong, claiming the dispute was with nearby St Michael's Cornhill and not neighbouring St Peter's.

The idea of a curse only appears in Kent's book. And was it the landowner, builder or architect who had the devils erected? Is the story true at all? The position of St Peter's is a strange one, with the entrance to the church squashed between offices and a sandwich shop for city workers. To our twenty-first century eyes, having places of commerce built into sacred places seems odd but it was common in the City in earlier times. An image of nearby St Ethelburga's Church on Bishopsgate, held at Bishopsgate Institute, shows shops built into the front of the church. At present, St Stephen's Walbrook and St Mary Woolnoth each have a Starbucks built into their flanks.

The Builder is a trade magazine for the building industry and lists every legal dispute to a building project, but does not mention St Peters or 54-55 Cornhill in its index over that period. The 1889–90 vestry minute book of St Peter Cornhill does list interactions between the church authorities and the architects of the current, devil-infested building, Walker & Runtz. They had recently acquired 54-55 Cornhill on behalf of a client, Mr Hugh H. Gardener, and they had found the original building to be 'somewhat shallow'. On October 1891 they wrote to St Peter's requesting a lease for 578ft of land where the old vestry building and lavatories stood, into which they could extend 54-55 Cornhill in exchange for £290 per annum. Walker & Runtz suggested that this money could be used to build a new vestry on another part of the site. After considerable discussion, the request was passed to the rector and churchwarden, who were 'of the opinion that no sufficient reason has been shown to justify them in recommending the scheme for the favourable consideration of the vestry'.

On 19 April 1892, Walker & Runtz served St Peter's with a party wall notice. Such a notice is given in a dispute over a boundary wall when it encroaches too far onto someone's property. The vestry were concerned enough to consider the cost of moving their wall back. So a dispute took place before the current 54-55 Cornhill was constructed; so far so mythical.

Walker & Runtz applied for the chance to buy 111.5ft of land to the west of the vestry, and this time the proposal was entertained. The money raised from the sale funded a new secure strong room for the church in which to keep their communion plate (before then a warden was taking it home to keep it safe) along with other improvements. After a meeting regarding the sale, the Ecclesiastical Commission made the decision to use the funds for the 'aid of the living'.

Pages 110–119 of the minute book have a report on the whole process of the sale, signed off by the rector on 25 October 1895. Once the Ecclesiastical Commission had approved the sale everything went smoothly: the Corporation of London approved it, and after the old building on 54-55 Cornhill had been demolished, the area of land was re-measured and sold. The report states that St Peter's has benefitted from the sale of ground that was previously used to keep lumber with its new strong room, improved lavatories and cloisters, as well as a fund to aid the living.

And that, as far as St Peter's minute book is concerned, is that, until 9 April 1901 when they received £150 for an increase in height of 54-55 Cornhill. There is no further mention of 54-55 Cornhill, and no mention at all of its devilish decorations.

✧ Enter the Ceramicist ✧

The man who sculpted the demons was William James Neatby (1860–1910). Neatby was an architect who turned to ceramics, creating some amazing tiles and building façades. He is most famed for the tiles entitled *The Chase*, which depicts various hunting scenes in the meat hall in Harrods, including speared ducks and captured boars. He could also do symbolic images, such as the *Spirit of Literature* on the front of the Everard Building in Bristol, a former print works. The spirit, in the form of a woman, has Guttenberg and his successor, William Morris, on either side of her. A grotesque dragon hangs from one drainpipe.

Neatby could also do the bizarre. The Turkey Cafe in Leicester is just that: his signature blending of Art Nouveau and Arts & Crafts-style ceramics with a regal turkey perched at the top, its tail feathers radiating from its rear like sunbeams.

Neatby is a fascinating and mostly forgotten figure, but he is often praised in architectural journals. In *The Studio,* J. Burnard enthuses about his 'vivid imagination a handicraftsmen who has thoroughly mastered the ways and means of his materials'.

Louise Irvine, writing in the *Architectural Review* in 1977, declared that 'many terracotta buildings in London and elsewhere reveal his influence and could even be him but, as yet, the necessary documentary evidence has not yet come to light'.

Neatby himself comes across as an enigmatic character; passionate but somehow severe. He could not see the point of impressionism and his style is a robust yet sensual combination of pre-Raphaelite, Art Nouveau, Art & Crafts and more. He used his first wife Emily, described as having 'delicate features and slender figure', as the model for his 'almost burlesque' tile decorations for the Winter Gardens in Blackpool. But Irvine twice tells, in different journals, the story that he was so jealous of other possible suitors for his wife that he kept her locked up at home with the blinds down.

Rather than a jobbing ceramicist for building exteriors, Neatby is often called an artist who is unable to express himself through his commissions, though another article suggests that *The Chase* was created so quickly for Harrods that he could not have consulted the client too closely. The devils on 54-55

Cornhill follow his trademark images that stop anyone looking at them in their tracks. They also resemble the grotesques he
created for the exterior of another London building, the Fox &
Anchor pub on Charterhouse. There are foxes on this stunning
building, described to me by a Blue Badge guide as London's
only Art Nouveau pub, but they have demonic faces and huge
yowling maws. They are more similar to the hyena-like creature
on Cornhill than a fox.

If not revenge, then why are there three devils on 54-55
Cornhill? One could answer 'why not'? Neatby was an eclec-
tic and evocative artist who, like other designers, decided to put
gargoyle-like creatures on one of the façades he was designing.
This was his first large piece in London and it is possible that
he would want to make a lasting impression. It is a credit to his
talent that the impression he makes is still so shocking.

✧ Demonic Cornhill ✧

If that explanation does not suit some, then I can offer some
speculation. Cornhill's fame as the highest point in the City may
have inspired Neatby, or the people who commissioned him, to
represent the bible story of the Devil tempting Jesus by taking
him up high and offering him the world. Perhaps the top demon
on 54-55 Cornhill is the Devil waiting on the highest peak to
tempt others.

Cornhill has its own demonic history too. There is a satanic
legend attached to the previously mentioned St Michael's
Cornhill, retold in the *Reader's Digest* book *Folklore, Myths and
Legends of Britain*, of a stormy night in the sixteenth century and
a group of bell-ringers who were horrified by an 'ugly shapen
sight' that floated through one window and over to another.
The bell-ringers fainted and awoke to find claw marks in the
stonework which became known as the Devil's claw-marks.

This devilish calling card was annihilated in the Great Fire of London, but it may be that Neatby was referring to this legend with his sculptors. There are also rumours that the self-styled devil worshipping decadents of the Hellfire Club met in the nearby George & Vulture eating house. This side of Cornhill has enough satanic geography for any myth-maker or rogue Blue Badge guide to weave a spooky story.

The problem in trying to prove that something did not happen is that evidence for a non-event is a tenuous and circumstantial thing to try and find. It's like investigating a crime that may not have happened by looking for a gun that is not smoking. It is almost certainly true that the demons of Cornhill are a striking piece of decoration and nothing more; they were not put there as any sort of revenge. The nearest thing I have found to a non-smoking gun on this is an illustration of 54-55 Cornhill which appeared in 29 June 1894 issue of *The Architect*. It is an architect's drawing of the building, giving it the name 'Tudor Chambers', published after its completion but not from life. The devils on the top and corner of the building are not the robust and grotesque creatures we have now, but winged, dragon-like beasts which are small and unimposing compared to Neatby's devils. This would suggest that Runtz, the architect and so the person with the biggest axe to grind against St Peter's Church, did not plan to have monsters gazing down on to the building. It was the talented ceramicist he employed for the façade that created the demons, for show rather than revenge.

✧ Satirical Stone Faces ✧

I have a friend who lives on Telegraph Hill, who is a keen local historian of south-east London. One night in the pub he told me that the stone faces carved over all the houses on the hill were representations of the German Royal Family. This did make some sense; the houses on the hill were almost all built between 1877 and 1899 when London had a large German community, many of whom were labourers. Perhaps when faced with hundreds of identical houses to erect, with space for an individual carving, a German stonemason or two couldn't resist chiselling a caricature of the monarchs from home. My friend, known as Neil Transpontine after his blog, sipped his beer again and completed the tale: during the anti-German riots at the start of the First World War, many of these stone faces were defaced by the angry English mob. This is why some houses on Telegraph Hill are missing their royal heads.

I left the story there, until a few years later I found a similar story in Peter Jackson's *London is Stranger than Fiction*. The entry for 22 February described the southern turret of St Giles' Church in Camberwell. St Giles' is the parish church of Camberwell and the architect of the building was Gilbert Scott. The turret bore gargoyles that were said to represent the political figures Lord Randolph Churchill, Gladstone, Lord Salisbury and Lord John Russell, as well as the politician and abolitionist William Wilberforce. I used to live opposite St Giles' but never noticed these carvings, so I went back to take a look. They may well have been public figures, but now time and rainfall have worn them, and their legend, away. I asked the vicar of St Giles', the Revd Nick George, about them but he knew nothing of the carvings or their history. He did enjoy the interesting story though.

Another stone grotesque with a story to tell is the 'hideous head of an old woman' on the right-hand side of the second window of the western outer wall of Mitcham parish church. The story, collected in James Clark's *Strange Mitcham*, tells of how the mason carving the corbels to support the church's windows had to do so with constant criticism from an old local woman. Eventually, the old woman found herself immortalised in stone by the mason.

Author William Kent's description of the urban myth origin of the Cornhill Devils is the second earliest after Peter Jackson's. Kent wrote at least a dozen books on London and in *The Lost Treasures of London*, a 1947 walk through the post-Blitz streets, he recounts a similar story to the Cornhill Devils that is linked to St Luke's Church on Old Street: 'It has sometimes been known locally as "lousy St Luke's" from a tradition regarding the weather vane. The story goes that the builder, peeved by "parsimonious treatment", placed a representation of a louse on the top of the tower.'

Kent went with a pair of field glasses and was 'inclined to accept the story'. This does not make the whole story true, however. Returning after the war to the bomb-damaged church, he noted that the louse was now gone, and presumed it had been taken during the war for its metal. The website for the London Symphony Orchestra, who now use the renovated St Luke's as a venue, has a contradictory quote about the weather vane from local resident John Mason: 'On top of the church there's a brass vane, and people in the area thought it was a louse, that's why they call it Lousy St Luke's … When they took it down I had a look at it; it had a beautiful red eye. After all these years the truth has come out – it's a dragon.'

The story of the revenge of the architect, stonemason or builder who hides an insult in the building he is designing or constructing has travelled across central and south London. It can be used to explain something strange or striking about buildings such as an extra-ugly stone carving, gargoyles with familiar faces or a weather vane that looks like an insect. That the story is best known around the Cornhill Devils is a testament to their visual power and their overbearing presence in such a bustling location.

10
THE MISADVENTURES OF BRANDY NAN

QUEEN ANNE (1665–1714), who reigned from 1702 to 1714, is best known for being the last Stuart monarch; the first monarch who had to deal with a two-party parliament system; being monarch during the Act of Union; lending her name to a style of table; and her romantic friendship with Sarah Jennings. In her own time she was known for a different perceived vice: she was known to love a drink and stories were spread of her hiding brandy in a teapot to disguise the amount she drank. She even gained the nickname 'Brandy Nan' for her love of the spirit. In 1712 a statue was erected of her, standing in front of the main entrance to St Paul's Cathedral to commemorate its completion in the ninth year of her reign and, presumably, greet arrivals to St Paul's. Grand intentions are often muddied by the irreverent and, according to the tale, the drink-loving queen's statue was gazing across the road at a pub. A rhyme was composed and scrawled on the statue which went:

Brandy Nan, Brandy Nan, they left you in the lurch,
With your face to the gin shop, your back to the church.

Meanwhile, in Salt Lake City, a bronze statue was erected to Mormon pioneer Brigham Young, standing with his back to the Mormon temple and his hand stretched out toward a bank. In an essay on Mormon humour it is suggested this mistake, if it was a mistake and not another sly designer's comment, provokes a sort of self-deprecating humour amongst Mormons who are required to tithe one tenth of their income to the Church. And that perhaps Young and other elders were more interested in the money of the Church of Latter-day Saints, and that LDS actually stands for 'lay down your silver'. There is even a rhyme that goes with the statue:

There stands Brigham, like a bird on a perch.
His hand to the bank and his back to the church.

In his book *Curses! Broiled Again!*, Jan Harold Brunvand repeated the Brigham Young song and also found a statue of Scottish poet Robert Burns in Dunedin, New Zealand, standing in The Octagon, the city centre plaza, with his back to St Paul's Anglican Cathedral and facing the 'commercial section of the city'. He correctly writes that he suspects there are more of the same legends elsewhere. I suppose it makes sense not to have a statue facing into a church with its back to arrivals, and with the famous figure looking outwards on to the material world, there is bound to be something inappropriate and unsuitable for their gaze to fall upon. I think it is human nature to comment on the juxtaposition between the two, but the rhyme that links Queen Anne and Brigham Young is a curious one, without pointing out that this must be the only thing linking these two historical figures. I would say the Salt Lake City rhyme follows the London one, though I have not found conclusive evidence for this, and I am sure any book on Salt Lake City urban legends may beg to differ. The Queen Anne statue is older, however: Brigham's bronze went up in 1847 and I am inclined to think that this urban legend migrated from England to America in this instance and not the other way around.

The earliest reference I can find to the 'Brandy Nan' rhyme is from an article of royal nicknames from the *Northern Echo* on 12 May 1896, which tantalisingly says that 'readers will remember the following lines which a wit of questionable taste bestowed on [Queen Anne's] statue'. The rhyme was well known enough to make it into *Brewer's Dictionary of Phrase & Fable*, published in 1898.

The original statue did receive a lot of abuse aside from insulting poems. In September 1743 the *Universal London Morning Advertiser* described the release of John Vaile, who had spent time in an asylum for breaking off the statues sceptre. 'Notes & Queries' from 11 April 1857 remembers that an arm was knocked off the statue in 1780, and was rumoured to have been done by a drunken man (though it may just have fallen off.) It notes that 'the statue of Queen Anne in St Paul's Church Yard seems endowed with the undesirable power of provoking the malice of iconoclasts'.

People still couldn't leave the statue alone in the 1960s, as a *Daily Telegraph* story from 20 October 1967 states that the statue is still 'a persistent target for vandals and over the years has been robbed of limbs, fingers, orb and sceptre.'

The statue of Queen Anne now has a fence running across her plinth and stands in peace; the only real indignity delivered to her now is how often she is mistaken for that other slightly stout female monarch, Queen Victoria.

✦ Brandy Nan on the Prowl ✦

The iconoclasts had better watch out. Way west of St Paul's, over on Queen Anne's Gate just off St James' Park, is another statue of Queen Anne that has an even stranger story attached to it than that of a boozy poem and a connection to a Mormon leader. In this quiet corner of affluent London, on the anniversary of Queen Anne's death – 1 August – the statue gets down from its pedestal and walks up and down the road.

The earliest version of the statue moving that I have found was in a cartoon by Peter Jackson for the *Evening News*. A later version, in the *Reader's Digest* book *Folklore, Myths and Legends of Britain* is the source for paranormal researcher James Clarke's account in his book *Haunted London*. James' account has the addition of the statue's promenade taking place on the stroke of midnight of the anniversary of the queen's death which, he told me, came from the guide of a walking tour he had taken. Always a reliable source.

Everyone loves the terrifying thought of statues coming alive. The earliest account I could find that may relate to Queen Anne's statue moving is from *Return of Outdoor Memorials in London* and reads as follows: 'The children of the locality were accustomed in their play to call upon the statue, by the name of 'Bloody Queen Mary', to descend from its pedestal, and on receiving, naturally, no response, to assail it with missiles.'

This does not sound to me like an account of a walking statue, but of a game played by children. There may be other and earlier stories of the Queen Anne statue walking around that the compiler of *Returns* may not have known about, but the children did. Or perhaps it was a game children played before pelting the statue, and the story grew from misreadings of this account and similar ones. But where did the story of the statue moving on an auspicious date come from?

Western Europe's landscape is littered with stone circles, lines of stones and other clusters of stone left from our Neolithic past.

At present, these are places of fascination; tourist sites that, for some, hold some ancient peace and wisdom within their bulk and patterns. Earlier peoples had a terror of these giant stones lying on the land and formed different stories of magic to explain them. So the Bulmer Stone in Darlington turns nine times at midday, while the stones that make up the circles of Nine Maids of Belstone Tor and Merry Maids of St Buryan are in fact petrified women who danced on the Sabbath. All of these legendary stones move at some point in time – at cock's crow, at midnight, at midday, on Midsummer Eve or Midwinter Eve or some other time. There are at least three hundred accounts of stones or stone circles moving at a liminal time, like the change of one day to another for Queen Anne, and the legend has managed to make its way from the countryside and into Westminster to attach itself to the statue. This may have been unconscious, as folklore, or conscious, by attaching an older myth to a new object. That statues move like megaliths has also made its way to Bloomsbury, where a recent tale emerged about the stone lions sitting outside the north entrance of the British Museum. Be there at midnight and you will see them stand up and stretch. Ideas are more durable than stone: even before statues wear away, their meaning can become lost and confused but ideas can breed and evolve amongst human humour, wit, error and fear, and can travel in the breath and letters of everyone.

PLAGUE PITS

The Black Death has entered London's folk memory as a founding
urban myth; every pothole in the road, every bump in a tube journey,
every square or roundabout seems to have a plague story attached to it.

♦

Richard Barnett, Sick City: Two Thousand Years
of Life and Death In London

WHEN I FIRST moved to the capital I lived in south-
west London. I was told that nearby Mortlake had
gained its name from the time of the Great Plague.
The bodies of plague victims had been sunk into the lake which,
forever more, was known as 'The Lake of the Dead': Mort-lake.
I was not the only new arrival to London to hear about the city's
burial sites for plague victims. A friend fresh from the north
west of England and new to south-east London was told that
she would need inoculating before going up to the giant plague

pit that is Blackheath. Even after decades here it feels like a step cannot be taken in London without crushing someone's bones, and a journey cannot be made without passing by, or through, a plague pit.

Clear pieces of land in the overcrowded city are thought to be where plague pits sit and seethe in the landscape. A work colleague and I were discussing this, and he told me that the 'small green on Caledonian Road and Wynford Street is on the site of a plague pit. That's why it was never built on.' He was told this in the early 1970s when he started a job in that area.

These mass graves are too dangerous to dig into or build over; infection may be lurking beneath the soil waiting for fresh air and a fresh chance to infect people. I read on a web forum that if there is an oval bulging out of an otherwise straight alley behind a line of Victorian houses, it is because there is a plague pit there. These could be seen on maps of nineteenth-century Tottenham, Stoke Newington and Islington before twentieth-century developers blundered over them.

Mount Pond on Clapham Common is a plague pit, as is the triangular piece of land where Champion Hill meets Denmark Hill in Camberwell. Horniman Triangle, the field opposite the Horniman Museum, is a plague pit. The roundabout on the corner of Gypsy Hill and Allen Park is a pit. In Norbury in the 1980s there was a protest against plans to put storage containers on a piece of land thought to be a plague pit.

They are not just a suburban danger, however. In his book *Underground London: Travels Beneath the City Streets*, Stephen Smith mentions that the Harvey Nichols basement menswear department has a low ceiling as the building cannot be dug any deeper into the ground, for fear of disturbing a pit. In the 1970s and '80s the London Folklore Group's newsletter, *London Lore*, told of an international bank with an office in the City on Gracechurch Street whose employees thought it was built over the graves of plague victims. The building had its own water supply, which some of the workers in the bank would refuse to drink for fear of infection.

The London Underground has to curve around, drop under or plough straight through the assembled subterranean plague victims previously left in peace. The 1972 *Reader's Digest* book *Folklore, Myths and Legends of Britain* lists a tale about the Bakerloo line whilst on the way to St John's Wood from Baker Street. This is now part of the Jubilee line. There is a point between the stations where the ears of passengers 'pop' as the tube tunnel drops to dip underneath a plague pit which sits beneath the Marylebone war memorial. The Piccadilly line between Knightsbridge and South Kensington stations has to bend around Brompton Oratory to avoid a plague pit. Bank station, in the heart of the City, is built on a plague pit or at least will stink 'like an open grave' from fumes wafting up from the pit Liverpool Street station is built into. The Victoria line cut through a plague pit under Green Park in the 1960s, and according to Mike Heffernan on the Unexplained Mysteries website: 'A huge tunnel-boring machine ploughed straight into a long-forgotten plague pit at Green Park, traumatising several brawny construction workers on site.'

Stephen Smith reveals why Muswell Hill does not have a tube station: 'They started to dig a tunnel there and hit a plague pit!' One can also find on the internet the answer to the mystery of why there are far fewer tube stations in south London: because of endless pockets of dead plague victims. Tube drivers using the southbound escape tunnel for runaway trains on the Bakerloo line between Lambeth North and the Elephant and Castle must take care to not hit the end too hard, as a plague pit lies just beyond the walls at the end of the line.

✧ Blackheath ✧

Blackheath is an open windy space above Greenwich. Despite greater London enveloping all sides of the heath, it does still have a desolate beauty. Houses cluster all along the edge of the hill Blackheath sits on but they avoid the top of it because, according to lore, Blackheath gets its name from being a plague pit for Black Death victims, just as Mortlake is the lake of death. In his book *And Did Those Feet: Walking Through 2000 Years of British and Irish History*, Charlie Connolly, remembers: 'I grew up in Blackheath in south London, to the casual observer just a great big expanse of grass sliced by a couple of roads. Yet it was a plague pit: during the Great Plague of 1665-6, hundreds of bodies were thrown into pits, scattered with lime and buried.'

Connolly demonstrates part of the attraction to plague pit urban legends here: that the storyteller has hidden knowledge they can share. He can lift the veil from an everyday piece of waste ground or greenery and describe the horror and history behind it. There is a dark glamour there.

On 7 April 2002, Blackheath Hill collapsed with a huge hole appearing across the A2 road so severe it took two years to repair. Remembering the event, a writer on the Tube Professionals Rumour Network website wrote that there was a 'big fuss' as Blackheath is 'another plague pit'. The fuss about the big hole in the A2 was really about the big hole running across a major road. What had collapsed was not a burial pit but the cavern that runs underneath Blackheath and Blackheath Hill. Discovered in 1780, these connecting caverns are thought to be chalk pits or hiding places dug by locals during the Danish wars. They run along and under Blackheath Hill from Maidstone Hill. They are known as 'Jack Cade's Cavern' in local lore, as it is thought the rebel leader Jack Cade hid in them to escape oppressive soldiers. Tours were given from 1850 and, after chandeliers were installed, balls were held in the caverns. They were abandoned in 1853 after a panic, when the lights went out. The caverns were next investigated in 1938 as a possible air-raid shelter. They were found unsuitable and were again sealed and forgotten about until the A2 caved in.

Blackheath is not a plague pit, its name being in use since at least the twelfth century, more than 500 years before the Black Death arrived in Britain. 'Blackheath' is thought to have come from the dark colour of its soil or have evolved from its description as a bleak heath. People are very fond of digging on the heath: as well as whoever dug the chalk pits, Blackheath, like much common land, was used by locals to dig gravel. After the Second World War these gravel pits were used to bury rubble from the Blitz which were then grassed over, causing the heath to lose its rugged, gorse-covered appearance and become the grassy flat space we know today.

The part of Blackheath that survived being built on – much of it didn't – was not because of the dead beneath it, but the living defending their piece of land from enclosure and development.

History being the weird, vast and diverse thing it is, of course, I will have to confess to you that there may still be a burial pit on Blackheath. Between 300-2,000 Cornishmen are in a mass grave somewhere on the heath. These men did not die as victims of the plague, but were killed by soldiers. They were camped up on Blackheath in 1497 on a march to London to protest against the taxes levied by King Henry VII to finance his war with Scotland. Henry sent in the troops and the Cornish rebels got no further than the heath. Local lore speculates that their bodies are buried beneath a mound called Whitfield's Mount. This may or may not be true.

The vast majority of burials in London are not related to the Black Death. However, the idea of the mass, unmarked pits still has such a hold over some imaginations that when we are hurtling through underground London it is always plague victims that keep us company down there.

✧ Green Park ✧

I have found little written down about London's plague pits out-side of repeated pieces of urban legends and the odd ominous nod toward a plague pit in the countless 'Haunted London' and 'Ghosts of London' books. Ghost books will use anything, like any good story-spinner, to set the right atmosphere for their tale. So the stories of the London Underground tunnel meet-ing a plague pit is in little threads across books, the internet and folklore. One of the clearer stories has already been quoted: the tunnelling of the Victoria line that disturbed a plague pit, while others say that the Jubilee line had to be redirected around a pit under the park.

It is a sign of the poisoned ground of Green Park that flowers will not grow there and, like Blackheath, has a sense of bleakness about it made all the stranger and unsettling for its location in the centre of London. Peter Underwood described Green Park's 'still-ness, an air of expectancy, and a sensation of sadness' in his book *Haunted London* and James Clark mentions the park's 'subdued atmosphere' in his London ghost book, also called *Haunted London*.

There may well be diseased bodies under the turf of the park, but they are not plague victims. Before the Reformation, the site of St James's Palace was a leper hospital; and this part of its history may have informed the plague myths of the park. The Victoria line, being the first deep tunnel line on the London Underground, does not see daylight at any point. This may also have stoked fears regarding what was down in the earth with the commuters. This has always been a fear related to subterranean travel: when an underground train line was first proposed for London, Dr Cuming held an open-air meet-ing at Smithfield preaching the apocalypse: 'The forth-coming end of the world would be hastened by the construction of underground railways burrowing into the infernal regions and thereby disturbing the devil.'

King Edward I granted the leper hospital the right to finance itself with an annual May Fair, so giving Mayfair, now one of London's richest areas, its name from an annual charity festival for lepers. Green Park is the former grounds of this London leper colony. Henry VIII, during his marriage to Anne Boleyn, claimed the site for the Crown and St James's Palace was built on the site of the hospital. The grounds were transformed into St James's Park, with the neighbouring ground called Upper St James's Park. However, this very ground (now known as Green Park) bears the mark of its history – flowers will not grow there. There are many theories as to why this is: flowers will not grow there because of the sad virgin leper girls buried beneath it; or perhaps it is because when the hospital was taken by the Crown, Henry VIII had the nuns of the hospital thrown onto the snowy ground of what is now the park. Some believe that there are no flowers in Green Park to mark heaven's displeasure with this cruel story from the Reformation. The irony is, that according to *Old and New London*, the leper hospital at St James's Park London was struck by the plague, which moved quicker than leprosy to take some of the inhabitants. None of this pestilent history has really affected the ground of Green Park however, because despite the lack of formal beds and gardens, narcissus flowers do bloom in Green Park in the spring.

◇ Down in the Ground ◇
Where the Dead Men Go

Contacting the Transport for London Corporate Archives, I was told that there are no specific references to plague pits in their records. They had just been through their archive to mark the 150-year anniversary of the London Underground and nothing came up. I wanted to make sure – plague pits really are everywhere in London lore – so I went through the files on the planning and construction of the Victoria line and the Fleet line, which became the Jubilee line, under Green Park.

The digging of the Victoria line is described in some detail in a pamphlet which was given away free when it opened. Miners were employed to work a digging shield that churned through the earth, and then reinforced the tunnels with concrete or steel supports. It must have been uncomfortable and claustrophobic and if they had met with bodies down there, it would have been just as unpleasant as the urban legend describes.

There were no references in the archives to this work uncovering dead bodies. The nearest possible reference I found to the plague was a note stating that there would always be the disinfectant Dettol with the workers constructing the Fleet line.

The plague pits of London are not lost and are not waiting to vomit up the dead onto unsuspecting builders and tunnel diggers. They are mostly well-mapped and their reality is every bit as unsettling and surprising as the urban myths. The mass graves were mainly dug for plague victims during the hottest, highest point of the Great Plague in August 1665. Before then, victims were buried in churchyards or in the grounds of pest houses (specially contained homes for isolating plague sufferers). Carnaby Street is near the sites of two seventeenth-century burial grounds for St James's workhouse. These sites, full and closed by 1733, may have been used as plague pits in the swinging 1660s. Carnaby Street has also been reported as the site of a pest house, the gardens of which extend out across Golden Square and Wardour Street. Maitland, in his *History of London*, reported that 'some thousands of corpses were buried that died of that dreadful and virulent contagion'.

Beneath the green grass of Charterhouse Square lies part of three pits which dealt with many of the dead. The oldest part, used in 1349, covers the area between Great Sutton Street and Clerkenwell Road. It was known as No-Man's-Land when purchased by the Bishops of London for burying plague victims.

The site runs from Clerkenwell Road down to Charterhouse and then into the top of Smithfield. The pits contain an estimated 10,000 bodies. Charterhouse Square has its own plague legend: apparently the schoolboys of Charterhouse School would dare each other to crawl across the square at midnight, when the groans and cries of the dead below could be heard.

The Devonshire Square development in the City is built on a pit once dug into a green field at the upper end of Hand Alley, according to Defoe, as was Hollywell Mount in Shoreditch, which is now a car park. Liverpool Street station and the Broadgate Estate are built on a pit open from 1569 until 1720, which was used for plague victims and other burials. There are two plague pits in the grounds of St Paul's Church, Shadwell; a pest-field (where plague victims were buried in large numbers) in the 'additional ground' of St John's Church Wapping, Whitechapel, had three pits, and St Bride's, off Fleet Street, had a pit which was closed halfway through the 1665 Great Plague. This may be why St Bride's sits so high above the ground. Marsham Street, Horseferry Road and Vincent Street cover a pit which was once part of Tothill Fields in Westminster, Golden Square and the multi-storey Soho car park on Poland Street. Famously, Bunhill Fields, just on the outskirts of the City, was another pit. The 'great plague pit in Finsbury' is under a car park and residential gardens for flats on the corner of Seward Street and Mount Mill. Lille Street Mansions, Normand Park and Fulham Swimming Pool sit on the site of the Lillie Road Pest Field.

There may not be a plague pit stopping the construction of a tube line to Muswell Hill, but a graveyard did prevent the building of houses there. The Queen's Wood was previously known as 'Churchyard Bottom Wood', being the site of an old church burial ground. In 1893 the Ecclesiastical Commissioners planned to sell off some of the wood for development, but local outrage prevented the building – which was sealed with the Highgate Woods Preservation Act of 1897 – going through parliament, allowing the wood's preservation through purchase. There must be many stories like this to explain why a tube line travels a certain way. In reality the older tubes followed the road layout so they could avoid building foundations, basements and crypts, not plague pits. Legal considerations can also affect a tube tunnel's direction. During the construction of the Fleet line, Transport for London set aside millions of pounds for dealing with lease holders who may not have been happy with a train running under their land.

✧ The Pits ✧

What of the suburban plague pits of Mortlake, Forest Hill, Camberwell, Muswell Hill and all the other sites? It is fair to say that when telling an urban legend, people never consider resources and logistics. With up to 4,000 people dying a day during the worst month of the Great Plague, Londoners did not have the time or energy to cart the wagons of the dead out into the countryside. Until the Great Plague, most plague victims were either buried in their local churchyards or in the grounds of the pest houses where plague sufferers had been confined. These pits are on the outskirts and edges of London (as it was then) and it would have been a huge waste of time and effort to drag the plague wagons out across the countryside to deposit the thousands of dead in Muswell Hill, Camberwell, Forest Hill, Blackheath and beyond. They had no need; the boundaries of the city at that point were on the edge of the City of London and Westminster, Wapping and Shadwell, which is where the dead were buried. In her book *Necropolis: London and Its Dead*, Catherine Arnold suggests that these legends sprung up after plague victims escaped London and wandered into the countryside of Camberwell and Forest Hill. The rural Surrey folk were familiar with what to do with infections, from their experience of murrain amongst their cattle, and the bodies of plague victims were dragged into holes by long poles and buried. The place of their burial, Arnold speculates, becomes a site of local lore.

People have dug up the dead. With London's long and populous history it would be very strange if digging up the city did not disturb some of the dead. There are still clusters of bones across central London, and often when they are found, the first thought is always that a plague pit has been discovered. This was the belief when bones were dug up in the Main Quad of University College London in 2010. After examination, the 7,394 bone fragments, 6,773 of which were human, were discovered to have a different story. Many of the bones had been cut by saws and scalpels, and many had numbers written on them. The burial was not a fourteenth-century plague pit, but parts of bodies buried there 100 years ago. The date of their burial was traced through a large Bovril jar that was buried with them, and it became clear that they were anatomy specimens that had been disposed of in a pit.

In April 2011, tunnel digging for the new across-London Crossrail line dug up hundreds, if not thousands, of bodies next to Liverpool Street station. These were not plague victims but inmates of the original St Bethlehem Hospital, the asylum known as Bedlam, who were buried in the churchyard.

SUBTERRANEAN SECRETS

12

Folk-lore means that the soul is sane, but that the universe is wild and full of marvels. Realism means that the world is dull and full of routine, but that the soul is sick and screaming.

✦

G.K. Chesterton

BETWEEN THE TUNNELS used by amorous and criminal historical figures, and the legends set within the London Underground, are other tales of underground London. The city is so honeycombed with basements, nuclear bunkers and tunnels that it must often ring hollow beneath the feet of its inhabitants. The unseen world is one full of allure, and a natural habitat for secrets.

✧ The Secret of the Elephant and Castle ✧

Waiting for a bus at the Elephant and Castle on a cold and rainy night must be one of the unspoken rites of passage of contemporary London, like seeing a cast member of *EastEnders* in the West End or realising that something being 'pop-up' doesn't automatically make it exciting. The asymmetrical jumble of the Elephant and Castle shopping centre, all dirty glass and faded pink plastic, is a strange, sometimes fascinating place. Was it really thought that putting it there would improve the area and the lives of those that inhabit it? 'No', according to writer Nigel Pennick, who believes that the shopping centre was constructed in the 1960s as a cover. In the 1940s an extension of the Jubilee line down to Camberwell Green was planned, before losing out in 1961 to the Victoria line running to Brixton. A mile or so of tunnel was dug and then abandoned, but not without an anarchist group noticing and describing it in their pamphlet *London – The Other Underground* as a 'government tunnel' linked via other secret passages to the City and Victoria. Pennick decided that during the 1950s, with the chill of the Cold War and fear of nuclear war in the air, these tunnels were converted into nuclear shelters, suggesting that many 1960s redevelopments were a cover for the construction of secret government bunkers. How does one cover up a secret underground government bunker near to Westminster but beneath a disreputable part of south London? You build a giant shopping centre as a cover and hope anarchists and authors do not notice. And that, some say, is why the Elephant and Castle shopping centre is there.

There are people that think that the government still has the power to have secret tunnels and sites across London, and there are endless rumours of a secret tube line for ferrying the Royal Family out of Buckingham Palace in the event of an attack or disaster. These are not new rumours; in 1914 a discussion on the drainage tunnels that run under Greenwich Park gave them the more heroic role of being a possible escape tunnel for Henry VIII, their kinks and bends there to perturb arrows that may be chasing the king as he squeezed down them. Another royal escape route is through the trees in St James's Park. They were arranged during the Second World War, somehow, to ensure that a light aircraft could land in the park to whisk the Royal Family out of Buckingham Palace should Germany successfully invade. This is what I was told by a friend in the Hermit's Cave in Camberwell anyway, but the friend who told me is a bit of a trickster – we were there to discuss his role in the Brentford Griffin hoax.

The MI6 building, Vauxhall Cross, on the south bank of the Thames, has a tunnel running from its basement to Vauxhall station, but in greater dangers it is rumoured that the building has a more drastic self-defence mechanism. Folklorist Martin Goodson found himself on the No. 36 bus going from Peckham to Camberwell and overheard three Camberwell art students talking:

> You know that in case of emergency I've heard that it (MI5 building) [actually MI6], can sink down and go under the river.'
>
> General hilarity broke out from the other students.
>
> 'No, it's true, it can. I've also heard it can turn black so that it cannot be attacked at night.
>
> The level of hilarity increased, but the student persevered in her conviction that this building is now equipped with some spectacular special effect qualities to protect itself in case of attack.

THE CORPSE ON THE TUBE

I slept with faith and found a corpse in my arms on awakening;
I drank and danced all night with doubt and found her a virgin
in the morning.

◆

Aleister Crowley, *The Book of Lies*

◇ Dead Line ◇

The best and most popular place to share an urban legend is some point during an idle chat. During a quiet moment, a work colleague mentioned a story her friend had told her about the London Underground. Someone, a friend of a friend or someone a bit further removed, had been travelling on the Underground late at night – she didn't know which line – in an empty carriage when three people got on and sat opposite her. Two men sat either side of a pale, limp woman. The half-remembered story, as it came across the desks at work, had the traveller being warned away from the two men and their pale companion and for good reason: the woman was dead.

Other versions of the same story can be found on the internet. Web forums are like chatting in the pub or during a tea break at work, but one can converse with like-minded people across the internet. The Unexplained Mysteries forum created a thread in 2007 called 'The Girl on the London Underground', which began with a friend of a friend (an art student) travelling back to her campus from central London late one night. She was alone, except for one other person in the carriage, a man who looked to be in his thirties. Then, three new people board: two men and a woman. The art student decided that the trio looked like drug addicts and avoided making eye-contact with them. Then, the thirty-something man started acting strangely. He walked over to the student and behaved as if he knew her, asking, 'Hi, how are you? I've not spoken to you in a long time,' before leaning into her and whispering, 'Get off at the next stop.'

The student was wary of this, but did not wish to be left alone on the train with what she thought were three drug addicts, so she followed the man off the train and onto the platform. Once they were off the train, the man revealed to the student that the girl in the trio was dead; he had seen the two men drag her onto the train with a pair of scissors embedded in the back of her skull.

A similar story was collected via an anonymous email in 2003 by the Urban Legend Reference Pages, better known as 'Snopes'. This tale came from a work colleague of the sender, whose boyfriend knew or had heard about a girl who got on the tube and, not wanting to sit on her own, sat opposite the three other people in the carriage. Again, this was a woman flanked by two men. The girl started to read, but whenever she looked up the woman was staring directly at her. The girl ignored the stares and at the next station a man boarded the train, looked about the carriage and sat down next to her. This new man then whispered to the girl, 'If you know what's good for you, you'll get off at the next station with me.' Despite feeling threatened by this, the girl presumed there would be other people at the next station and got off. At this point the man revealed himself to be a doctor, who could tell that the staring woman was dead and the two men either side of her were propping her up.

❖ A Mystery on the Underground ❖

Another version of the previous tale takes place on an inter-city train. Two women travellers are stared at intensely by a girl who they find out later had been murdered by her two female companions. Could this be the same story, warped by whispered repetition, as the story Rodney Dale records in his book *It's True … It Happened to a Friend* (1984)? This version has a girl getting onto a quiet subway carriage and doing her crossword. A man gets on, whom she ignores, and then at the next stop two more men board and sit either side of the first man. As the train stops again, the two men get off, leaving the first man in his seat, although not for long. As the train jolts out of the station the man falls out of his seat with a knife in his back. This time the corpse on the tube becomes one right in front of our unfortunate commuter. The story takes place on the subway rather than the tube, so where could it have happened? I asked Rodney Dale if he could remember his source or the location for this version but sadly, it is a very small section in the book and he could not.

One possible origin for the corpse on the tube legend is a fictional story serial called 'A Mystery on the Underground' by John Oxenham, which appeared in *To-Day* magazine in 1897. Presented as fake newspaper clippings rather than a conventional narrative, the story begins with men turning up dead while travelling on the District line. Early on in the story, finding the body is like finding the corpse in one version of the urban legend in this book: a lone woman on the tube discovers a man is dead when his body falls off the seat as the train wobbles.

A story about this stroy claims the tube companies were concerned that people would mistake each episode for actual news clippings. There was a mocked-up cartoon, supposedly from *Punch*, showing shocked people on a crowded stagecoach when they hear a man is still taking the tube. The tube contacted the editor of *To-Day*, the famed writer Jerome K. Jerome, to complain. Jerome considered pulling the story but, having one more episode to go, which took place on a ship rather than the London Underground, Jerome let it run. There is no mention of any 1897 tube panics in *The Times* index for that year, and in his autobiography, Jerome does not discuss *To-Day* any further than his regrets when he had to sell it.

After the initial similarity to the corpse on the tube legend early on in the story, there is no further resemblance to it in 'A Mystery on the Underground'. The murders always take place on a Tuesday and the victims are shot dead in the carriage by an anonymous killer and not led on to the train by shifty characters. If a cause of death is mentioned in the urban legend, it is a stabbing.

✧ Death on the Tracks ✧

The story of the corpse on the tube is clearly an urban legend, but was it ever more than just a horror story about travelling with strangers in confined spaces? People do die on London's public transport; the TUBEprune, the Tube Professionals' Rumour Network, is a website full of gossip and stories, purportedly from London Underground staff. One section describes two instances when bodies have been found on the tube, though they do both have the air of a story rather than the retelling of an event. The first was when a train arrived at East Finchley station at the end of the morning peak time. The crew inspected the train and found a man slumped in a seat, who they tried to wake. They discovered that the man was dead, and had been for so long that rigor mortis had set in and he was rigid in his seat. The body had to be removed by being laid sideways on a stretcher to prevent it rolling off.

While rigor mortis begins three to four hours after death – so is possible after the morning peak – maximum stiffness does not set in until around twelve hours. It is possible the body was left overnight on the tube, but hopefully not.

Another find was on the eastbound Piccadilly Line at Northfields. A passenger raised the alarm when a man on the packed train seemed 'a bit poorly'. The guard did not wish to delay the train so he persuaded a couple of passengers to help him drag the corpse off the train and left it sitting upright on a bench. The police were called and complained about the disrespectful treatment of a body. The guard then responded with, 'What else could I do, I couldn't delay the train, could I?'

Whether this is a true story or not, or a joke about the far edges of job-worthiness told by TfL staff, or even a blending of the two, I shall leave up to you to decide. A problem that occurs when one spends a lot of time researching, writing and thinking about urban legends is that you end up doubting every story you hear unless the teller can show you photographs, official documents or the scars. And even then you still doubt.

One person who was almost certainly found dead on the tube was German naval lieutenant-commander and suspected Nazi spy, Franz Rintelen von Kleist. The former Isle of Man internee was found dead on a train at South Kensington tube station in May 1949.

THE STRANGER'S WARNING

That was the way with Man; it had always been that way. He had carried terror with him. And the thing he was afraid of had always been himself.

♦

Clifford D. Simak
Way Station

A DEADLY STRANGER LURKING in the back of a woman's car has not been the only warning to circle around the internet, purportedly coming from the Metropolitan Police. A fake message warning people not to travel on the London Underground emerged on 24 July 2005. The email claimed that controlled explosions had taken place around 15 July, at Piccadilly Circus and Leicester Square stations. They had not. Much like the fake warning of the stranger hiding on the back seat (*See* Criminal Lore) persons unknown were inventing police warnings.

The fear of the enemy amongst us, either terrorists or infiltrators, has haunted people for a long time and a particular sort of urban legend has accompanied these fears. In the twenty-first century, urban myths or rumours of the 'Helpful Terrorist' or 'Strangers Warning', have been spread quickly by email and internet forums. Our century has seen terrorist attacks across the world and these have left fear and folklore in their wake. Over the winter of 2001, an email warning of the possibility of an attack started popping into people's inboxes. Below is a typical version taken from the website Snopes.com. It arrived via the girlfriend of a friend of a relative of a friend – even farther removed than the standard 'friend of a friend':

Morning all,

Had a bizarre message from my brother in the early hours of this morning …

His friend's girlfriend was shopping in Harrods on the weekend. There was an Arab man in front of her who was buying a number of things with cash – he was a few pounds short so the girl offered him £3 to cover it.

He thanked her profusely and left. When she left the store the man followed her out and thanked her again and warned her not to travel on the tube today! [1 October 2001]. She was a little thrown by this so she went to the police. The police were very sceptical but in order to eliminate her suspicions gave her the photo-ID book of all known dissidents in the UK. He was on the second page listed as a known terrorist.

This is apparently true and the police are apparently taking this extremely seriously. The most likely time would be rush hour this evening so please avoid it if you can – who knows it may be nothing but is it worth the risk?

PS- I don't have a lot of people's e-mail addresses so obviously please forward this on to anyone and everyone.

I am certain that if the Metropolitan Police suspected that the London Underground was going to be bombed on a specific date, they would not leave it up to members of the public to spread the word via email.

The 'foaf' in this version of the urban legend is generally a woman, which may be because women are considered more kind; it has consistently been a woman throughout the legend's evolution.

The woman gives the mystery man £3 and warns of danger in London, with this legend it is typically the larger fee in London and a lesser fee of 68p at a cash and carry when Birmingham is the potential target for attacks. As well as the London Underground and Birmingham, warnings have been given regarding Coventry, Tamworth, Milton Keynes and Chester. This type of urban folklore has spread to America, with the warning given to a woman about drinking a popular brand of soft drink after 7 September. In an alternative version, a male waiter, after giving a customer change for the phone, is warned to avoid a second popular soft drink after 1 June.

Many tales of the 'Helpful Terrorist' have been borne from the sad events of 11 September 2001, including warnings from boyfriends to their girlfriends not to go near the World Trade Centre or the Pentagon on that day. The story of 9/11 was retrospective and so false but there was a warning for later that year: 'Don't go to any malls on Halloween'. It seems that many urban legends evolve from huge events and are subject to change as the story is carried from person to person.

✧ The Enemy Within ✧

One of the most disturbing urban legends covers the possibility of the enemy among us, that the person sitting next to us could be a terrorist, or the far more dangerous implication that a group of people living within our community are complicit in the actions of a terrorist cell. It seems unlikely, but some urban rumours have entire communities that are aware of terrorist assaults prior to the actual event.

These rumours can gather such momentum that city authorities have to release statements ensuring the public that they are untrue. Such is the nature of an urban legend, that the repeated telling can give a story credibility although it has no apparent basis in fact, nor any evidence to support it.

In New York, the police released an announcement in January 2003. 'There is no terror plot or threat connected to the rumor that is circulating in New York and in other cities abroad,' said Deputy Police Commissioner Paul Browne. This was apparently in response to a rumour that a cab driver had warned one of his female customers of an impending terror plot.

Snopes, an invaluable aid in gathering rumours, also related an earlier version of the stranger's warning legend. In 2000, a version of this story was circulating in Manchester in which a woman helps a young man out by lending him some money while in the queue of a fast-food restaurant. She is rewarded by being warned to keep out of a local shopping centre in March on that year in a soft Irish accent. The change in stranger is important: the is an urban legend that attaches itself to many different ethnicities.

The rumour of the helpful terrorist goes further back than this century and from terrorism to all out war. During the First and Second World War there were many strange and frightening rumours flying around London and the rest of the UK, and some that seem familiar today. Rumours of the enemy among us came in the shape of supposed fifth columnists walking our streets. At the start of the Blitz, there were fears that German agents were signalling to bombers circling London. One German-Swiss man in Kensington was arrested for smoking a large cigar: 'He was puffing hard to make a big light and pointing it to the sky,' said a witness who feared the smoker was in fact communicating with enemy bombers.

During the Battle of Britain, it was rumoured that Hermann Göring himself had flown in a bombing raid over London. By 1942, this had evolved into Göring being seen sitting in an air-raid shelter in Plymouth after parachuting in to watch the city being blitzed. Just as Adolf Hitler had his eye on London offices and flats and had visited the UK in his youth (*See* Nazis over London), Osama Bin Laden was often sighted in America after he became public enemy number one. He was usually seen in coffee shops or eating in fast-food restaurants.

The First World War was fertile ground for rumour and folklore, with stories of angels protecting British troops as they retreated from their first engagement at Mons. There was the hope of Russian allies travelling through Britain by train to reinforce the frontline. These warriors were identified by the snow on their boots.

Once the Great War began, bizarre rumours began to spread across the city. Concrete, patented in 1849, became a source of anxiety. Tennis courts were suspected of being secret German machine gun placements, and a factory in Willesden with views of the Crystal Palace that was constructed from concrete was raided by police in 1914, because it was discovered that it had another office located in Leipzig. The owner of Ewell Castle successfully sued the *Evening News* and the *People* after the newspapers published a story saying that their concrete-bottomed lake was being capable of mounting five heavy guns, which had the firepower to take out the main railway line into London. Evidence given for the castle owner being a spy included his expensive car. On 3 October 1914 the rumour led to the *Daily Mail* asking: 'Is it too much to ask that our kid gloved government will ascertain how many German owned factories have been built in this country which incidentally command Woolwich, Dover, Rosyth? A timely inspection might reveal many concrete structures.' Police led a futile search of the abandoned King William tube station when the *Railway Magazine* suggested there was a cell of enemy agents occupying the location and using it as a base to shoot and bomb their way across the city.

One night in October 1916, a Zeppelin was said to have descended onto Hackney Marshes and a tall man with an eye patch was lowered down in a basket. He got out, asked a couple of bystanders the way to Silvertown and they told him to follow the River Lea until he got to Bow. The man and the Zeppelin then disappeared into the night. The couple then informed the police.

Sir Basil Thomson, head of CID at Scotland Yard during the start of the First World War wrote an informative and entertaining book about his investigations from that time, *Queer People*. In the book, he tells a tale of a caddish German officer 'being seen in the Haymarket by an English friend; that he returned the salute involuntarily but then changed colour and jumped into a passing taxi, leaving his friend gaping on the pavement.' Other legends have a young girl meeting her fiancé who is an enemy officer in disguise. He forgets himself briefly greeting her with affection, before remembering himself and turning away. Infiltrators have revealed themselves in various ways, such as swearing to themselves in their native tongue.

Around the same time, a familiar story was spread. The following is from *Queer People*:

> The next delusion was that of the grateful German and the Tubes. The commonest form of the story was that an English nurse had brought a German officer back from the door of death, and that in a burst of gratitude he said at parting, 'I must not tell you more, but beware of the Tubes in April [1915].'

Basil Thomson tracked this rumour:

> We took the trouble to trace this story from mouth to mouth until we reached the second mistress in a London Board School. She declared that she had had it from the charwoman who cleaned

the school, but that lady stoutly denied that she had ever told so ridiculous a story.

The rumour appeared during the Second World War too, but this time the nurse was treating a captured German pilot and was rewarded for her kindness by being advised to carry her gas mask on 15 September. Did a rumour from the cleaner of an unnamed London Board School migrate almost entirely intact to the twenty-first century? Perhaps the reason the character in the tale is always a woman is because the original figure was a female nurse. It is clear that the person given the warning is kind and worthy of the advice. In fact, the latest version of the story does contain a role-reversal. After the shooting of Osama Bin Laden, Paris feared it would suffer reprisal attacks. In the Parisian version of May 2011, one man returns another man's wallet, and is rewarded by being advised not to use the Metro the following day. A legend being told at the same time sees one woman helping another by sparing some change for a parking meter near Carnegie Mellon University – she is told not to attend any rallies for the Tea Party.

Like the mugger hidden on the back seat of a woman's car, or dead eyes staring at you on public transport late at night, this urban myth relates to fear, prejudices or a blind spot in general knowledge where wild speculation can takes its place. The Strangers Warning relates to a very specific situation in which there is a threat of attack by persons unknown on civilians in an urban setting. It is bound within the fear of attack that the Helpful Terrorist story is able to pass from person to person as a truth, especially during times of great anxiety when emotions are running high and people want to believe in the good of a stranger.

The following is an interview with Alexander Walters, who served a term of one year in prison for a hoax bomb alert at Heathrow airport on 15 September 2001. On 26 November 2002, the *Guardian* reported:

He had been out walking his dog on September 15, when an urge suddenly seized him to phone Heathrow airport on his mobile.

'There is a bomb at the airport,' he told the operator. 'You have exactly one hour.' The call was traced to his phone – which, like him, was in south Wales.

What on earth was he thinking?

'I didn't think at all. I just went for a walk. It was just something that happened so fast that I didn't even know what I was doing until it was too late.

'It wasn't attention-seeking, it was just, I think, a way of letting anger out. I had one or two problems at the time, and obviously I did something really stupid.'

What was he angry about?

'I wouldn't know, it was just a spur of the moment thing. You just totally switch off and do something you shouldn't have done. And then before you know it has caused this huge thing.'

Is this what the author of a hoax email in thinking or feeling as he or she writes it?

◇ This Era's Enemy ◇

The Great Fire of London, now believed to have been an accident that started at a bakery in Pudding Lane, was long regarded as a piece of Catholic terrorism. Robert Hubert, a French watchmaker living in Romford, confessed to starting the fire, being an 'agent of the Pope' and taking a bribe from the king of France. England was also at war with Holland at the time of the fire and it was feared that 'the French and the Dutch have fire'd the City'. Despite concerns about his mental state, Hubert was hanged at Tyburn on 28 September 1666 for starting the fire, before it emerged that he had in fact arrived in London two days after the fire had begun. During the execution, an effigy of the Pope was burned with a head full of cats that screamed for the pleasure of the crowd as the flames reached them.

The Monument to the Great Fire of London at Fish Street had inscriptions blaming Hubert and 'Popish frenzy, which wrought such horrors, is not yet quenched', which were not permanently removed until 1830.

On Monday, 2 September 1666, the second day of the fire, a maid from Covent Garden called Anne English was arrested after she was reportedly claimed that a group of French men had delivered a warning to her master. The men told him to move his goods as 'within six weeks that house and all the street would be burned to the ground'. She was interrogated at Whitehall, but denied the story stating that she had heard 'that the French and Dutch had kindled the fire in the City.'

The helpful terrorist has an ancestor in a warning passed on before the Gunpowder Plot of 1605. Just before it's failed execution, there was a warning delivered to the Catholic Lord Monteagle who was having dinner in Hoxton when he received a letter pleading with him to 'shift of your attendance at this Parliament' as Parliament was due 'a terrible blow' on 5 November. This is not thought to be a genuine warning from one Catholic to another however. The origin of this warning is suspected to be from Monteagle himself who knew some of those involved in plotting an attack, but did not want to be seen to betray them. Another suggestion is that it was a secret service letter that was designed to be used as evidence against those plotting atrocities. Basil Thomson was a former intelligence officer who was sometimes involved in disseminating misinformation. Perhaps, this urban legend is a covert way of drawing information out of the public. Propaganda has been used as a tool for a long time, but once the story has been released, it is free to be adapted and moulded and is not easy to control. As well as planted rumour, there were hoaxers, liars, old prejudices, people who communicate their ideas through allegory and story, and the people who believe the stories and pass them on.

There is one more tale of an act of kindness gaining insight set in London but the knowledge is of a very different nature. Broadcaster, journalist and wit Nancy Spain (1917–1964) is reported to have seen a ghost on Piccadilly. Spain saw the ghost after she had just left Fortnum & Mason and was looking for a cab. One pulled up in front of her and a woman with red hair got out, fumbling in her purse. Spain was in a hurry and paid the fare for the elderly woman who then went into the store without saying a word. Once Nancy Spain was in the cab the driver said, 'You were caught there, Miss. That old gal could buy both of us. That was Lady C.' Speaking of the incident the next day, Spain was wordlessly given a newspaper by her mother that carried the headline, 'Lady C. Dies in Fire'. The knowledge Spain gained through her generosity was of the world of ghosts and not of terrorism.

Spain apparently saw ghosts in the strangest places; she once encountered the spectre of her friend Bin who had died at the age of twenty-four at a restaurant. Of the event she said, 'Once I am sure I saw her come into a restaurant. She sat down and ordered, of all things, a Scotch Egg. But when I leapt up to say hello she seemed to vanish, leaving a hard, clear line for a second, as a piece of paper does when it burns in the fire.'

The stranger's warning legend is the classic story of entertaining angels unaware, or the fairytale of a hero or heroine who gained the favour of god through an act of kindness. The story shows how kindness can be rewarded and has the hopeful note that an attack may be avoided.

15

NAZIS OVER LONDON

German airmen are careful not to bomb breweries and maltings in Britain because Hitler knows that if Britons go on drinking at the present rate, we shall lose the war.

✦

Unnamed clergyman from Chester and Warrington Methodist Synod quoted from The Tumour in the Whale.

THE GORDON RIOTS of June 1780, London's most violent protest, were inspired, or at least encouraged, by Lord George Gordon's speeches against laws proposing to allow the nation's Catholic citizens the right to buy land, practise medicine, teach and join the House of Commons or Lords. More fuel for the mob's fury came as a result of fearful rumours of 20,000 Jesuits hiding beneath tunnels under the Thames, waiting to take London on orders of the Pope, like the Germans lurking in King William Street Station (*See* p. 111) .

By 1914, in the prelude to the First World War, it was London's German community who had become the enemies within as London's most violent riots since the Gordon Riots destroyed German shops and homes. The 1914 issue of *The Railway Magazine* prompted a police investigation of the abandoned King William Street tube station after suggesting it was being used as a base and weapons store for German infiltrators.

⟡ The Nazis' Favourite Landmarks ⟡

The Blitz brought new stories. As people died and whole neighbourhoods were devastated, stories swirled around London landmarks to explain how and when they survived. Nelsons Column still stood because Adolf Hitler had taken an interest in it. On his successful occupation of London, he had planned to carry the symbol of British naval might to Germany as a way of underlining his victory.

The 1930s tower of Senate House, University of London's imposing base in Bloomsbury, survived because, according to Graham Greene, it was used as a marker for bombers approaching Kings Cross and St Pancras stations. Senate House was also earmarked to be the base Hitler planned to use as the German central office for ruling Britain after their invasion.

The 1937 Art Deco block of flats Du Cane Court in Balham is quite pleased of its reputation as Hitler's possible home or HQ in London. The Führer even placed spies within the building. Like Senate House, German air crews would use the Du Cane Court as a handy landmark: 'It was turn left at Du Cane Court and then head home for Germany.' Du Cane Court is proud enough of the legend to put the story up on its website but also sheepishly ponders whether the block's architecture may really have attracted the genocidal leader; but 'true or not, the flats were quite an innovation at the time'. Antony Clayton, in

The Folklore of London, uncovered stories that the architect of Du Cane Court was a Nazi sympathiser who planned to have the building make a swastika in the middle of South London when viewed from the air. This takes us back to the stealth swastika of the kindly prisoner-of-war German soldier and his gardening surprise (*See* 'The Hidden Insult' p. 22).

Some South London landmarks that were removed included the golden *Goddess of Gaiety* statue at the top of Wimbledon Theatre, which was taken down in 1940 and not replaced until 1992, as it was thought to be an excellent guide to German bombers. On the edge of London, and on the top of a hill, St Helier Hospital in Carshalton was painted black during the Second World War so it would not be used as a landmark for incoming German planes.

All of these landmarks fared better than the north tower of the ruined Crystal Palace. Having survived the fire of 1936, which destroyed the rest of the glass building, the tower was destabilised and blown up with dynamite in 1941 because many, including William Kent in his *Lost Treasures of London* book, thought it was being used as a navigation point for German bombers. Other reasons included to prevent it falling in a bombing raid; presumably a controlled explosion was safer, and the tower's steel was needed for the war effort. This was the line used in a British Pathé news film of the demolition, called *Crystal Palace Tower – The End*. People were sceptical about the gathering of scrap metal and park railings during the Second World War, thinking that the metal was not and could not have been used for weapons and vehicles. The collecting of metal was thought to be a morale-boosting exercise and the metal was used as ships' ballast, dumped in the Thames Estuary or taken out to sea to be dumped by Canning Town dockers in such great amounts that incoming ships had to be guided in by pilots because the quantities of metal were affecting their compasses.

Another building thought to be spared by the bombers was Winchester Cathedral, as the Nazi propaganda broadcaster Lord Haw-Haw was said to have gone to the school by the cathedral and had asked Field Marshall Goring to spare it in the raids. Another rumour told of Hitler planning to be crowned as king at Winchester Cathedral once Germany was victorious. A retort to the Winchester rumour said, 'Any Coronation dream would obviously have Westminster Abbey as its centre.'

The removal and camouflage of prominent landmarks was perhaps a sensible precaution before and during the Blitz. On the eve of the Second World War, London was preparing for sustained aerial bombardment and for mass burials, stocking up on cardboard coffins, for example; London County Council envisaged mass burials in lime pits. The predictions for an aerial bombardment on London were based on 700 tons of high explosive being released with the casualty rates of 175,000 per week. The destruction of towers, the removal of bright objects from theatres and painting landmark buildings black therefore seems feasible. The estimates were far greater than the actual, still terrible, death toll of the war: the total bombs dropped on Britain were an estimated 64,393 tons, killing 51,509 people.

There is another factor. The architecture of Du Cane Court and Senate House must have linked them to the Nazis and Hitler in the minds of frightened and angry Londoners. Ironically, Senate House was designed to symbolise the future world, having survived the First World War, and it was actually intended to be an international beacon of learning: 'It must not be a replica from the Middle Ages.' Perhaps these rumours of Hitler's interest evolved out of Londoners' suspicions at the modernism of the architecture of Du Cane Court and Senate House and their resemblance more to the Reichstag building than to the British Museum or Natural History Museum. With enemy planes flying overhead and spies rumoured to be everywhere, the Second World War must have felt like no other time to London civilians.

Perhaps all of these legends come from Londoners feeling enemy eyes directly on the landmarks of their lives.

✧ The One and the Many ✧

An earlier British folk tale took place in Dorset and was recorded in 1930. A West Lulworth man remembered a story told to him by a 104-year-old resident of the town, who apparently witnessed Napoleon arriving at Lulworth Cove in August 1804. He arrived at the cove with a companion seeking a place to land for an invasion, but was heard to mutter 'Impossible!' before 'folding his maps and returning to his boat'. Emperor Bonaparte personally taking the time out to inspect land sites on enemy territory seems as likely as Hermann Göring, commander of the Luftwaffe and Adolf Hitler's deputy, braving anti-aircraft fire to take a look over London.

Both stories have a possible origin in fiction. Thomas Hardy claimed to have invented Napoleon's trip to Dorset for a short story in 1882 and was amazed to hear the story repeated back to him by friends. Stories of Göring's midnight flights over London may have been inspired by a fake news report that Göring, who was an ace fighter pilot during the First World War, had piloted a plane over London on 15 September 1941 escorted by two bombers.

However, I think there may be more happening within these legends than just a misinformed regurgitation of fiction. Mother Teresa is quoted as saying, 'If I look at the mass I will never act. If I look at the one, I will.' She was thinking of human responses to suffering: people will give more for an individual rather than a group of people. We are interested in times of war. These stories reflect how people think and feel during a war with an invasive force.

With an event the scale of the Second World War, it would be impossible to imagine the thousands of troops involved in the planned attacks on us. To think of their equipment, how it is maintained and who supplies this aggressive organisation, it is far easier to look to the head of the enemy, the very top, and imagine them taking a very close personal interest in our homes, the beaches they could land on, the buildings they could live in. Somehow, this – Adolf Hitler picking his offices and deciding where he would be crowned – is far easier to imagine and respond to than one nation moving against another.

16

CRIMINAL LORE

Adults tell fairy tales, to adults, although the maudlinized
and castrated samples in print belie the fact.

✦

Richard Dorson, Folklore and Face

✧ Beware all Lady Drivers ✧

It is just before Christmas 2003 and Antony Clayton was checking his email. He found the following warning sent to him on
17 December with the subject line 'Danger when Filling Up at
Petrol Stations':

Beware all lady drivers. This is a West End Central Police Crime
Prevention information message providing details of local crime
and disorder issues. If you have information about any crimes
mentioned please contact the Crime Desk at West End Central

Police Station on … . We need your help to make Westminster a safer environment.

A woman stopped at a pay at a petrol pump station to get fuel. Once she filled her petrol tank and after paying at the pump and started to leave, the voice of the attendant inside came over the speaker. He told her that something had happened with her card. The lady was confused because the transaction showed complete and approved. She relayed that to him and was getting ready to leave but the attendant, once again, urged her to come in to pay or there would be trouble. She proceeded to go inside and started arguing with attendant about his threat. He told her to calm down and listen carefully. He said that while she was filling her car, a guy slipped into the back seat of her car on the other side and the attendant had already called the police. She became frightened and looked out in time to see her car door open and the guy slip out.

One would hope that warnings from Westminster police would not contain so many typographical errors and banal attempts at drama. The message concludes with a warning:

The report is that the new gang initiation thing is to bring back a woman and her car. One way they are doing this is crawling into the women's cars while they are filling with petrol or at stores at night-time.

Be extra careful going to and from your car at night. If at all possible do not go alone.

1. ALWAYS lock your car doors, even if you are gone for just a second.

2. Check underneath your car when approaching it and check in the back before getting in.

3. Always be aware of your surroundings and of other individuals in your general vicinity, particularly at night.

Antony Clayton got to the end of the warning and knew just what to do. An author of a number of books on London, including *The Folklore of London*, he submitted the dread message to the *Folklore Society News* (FLS News) and it appeared in Issue 43, June 2004. The legend itself spread, and arrived to a different reader pretending to be an email sent by Harrow Council Civic Centre which concluded: 'This is a real warning! The alert originated from a London company who had a female employee involved in the above instance.'

In some ways the gang member hiding in a woman's car has a similar plot to the corpse on the tube urban legend. A woman is travelling alone at night; she is in danger, but is unaware of it until a man distracts her by frightening or annoying her until she learns the truth.

There may be, along with the corpse on the tube, some subconscious concern or disapproval of women travelling alone in the urban night, with all its strange but very real dangers. Women are still thought of as more vulnerable than men, so to be plausible these stories may choose a lone woman as the target of the anonymous nocturnal predator.

This is a legend we share with America. Snopes has collected versions via email in 1999 and 2000, and in 2001 a version very much like the London one appeared, minus the Westminster police contact details but with the warning: 'THIS IS TOO SERIOUS … DO NOT DELETE. PLEASE PASS IT ON!!'

By 2004 the Dublin version named a gang, the 'Westies', who were carrying out these surreptitious attacks, and the message warned that the abducted woman would be taken at knifepoint and gang raped.

The gang initiation aspect is not part of the story yet, but it is easy to see how it became linked. The idea of gang initiation feeds many urban legends, the most popular being the warning to never flash your car headlights back if a strange car flashes them at you. The car has a would-be gang member inside who needs to murder the first driver to flash back at them in order to join. Snopes has a version of the story from 1999, where hidden gang members hamstring a woman and 'remove a body part' to gain entry to the gang. The victim is always a woman. In the 1998 version the attacker is a serial killer, still coasting on the 1990s wave of cultural interest in the mind of serial murderers which drew people to films such as *The Silence of the Lambs*. Despite Hannibal Lector still haunting the cinema and television, the fear of criminal gangs was soon to sweep the serial killer out of the popular imagination and out of this urban legend.

Like the male rescuer in the corpse on the tube legend, there is a suggested element of danger from the rescuer, until he speaks to the woman (in the earliest version he speaks to the woman's husband when she gets home but happily urban legends have moved on since 1967) and tells her of the dangerous stranger in the back of her car. In *The Vanishing Hitchhiker* (1983), Brunvald writes: 'In more imaginative sets of these legends the person who spots the dangerous man in the back is a gas station attendant who pretends that a ten dollar bill offered by the woman driver is counterfeit. With this ruse he gets her safely away from her car before calling the police.'

As we have seen in the early twenty-first century London version of this urban legend, with its faulty credit card, the story is the same but the props change over time.

⋄ Child Abductors through History ⋄

Another widely travelled abduction legend made it into the *FLS News* No. 37 June 2002 issue. Correspondent Susan Hathaway heard from a work colleague that his wife's 'friend's daughter's college friend' was the mother of a child who had gone missing in a John Lewis store near London. Security was alerted and all doors were sealed to ensure the child did not wander out of the building. A few minutes later the child was found emerging from the toilets with a different coloured dress, a new short haircut and a group of strangers herding her. The Mumsnet internet forum has a thread for sharing and disarming scare stories including this child-danger story. Locations for it included an east London Tesco, a Co-op on the Isle of Wight and other shops in Bristol, Tokyo or Gloucester.

An earlier pre-email version had a ten-year-old boy, not the more usual pre-teenage girl, being accosted in a shopping centre toilet by 'an ethnic gang of youths' and castrated. Another story has a teenage girl going to the toilet in the restaurant of a large shop only to not return after half an hour. As with the girl with the re-dyed hair, the daughter is found just in time as she is being dragged unconscious out of the loo by two 'husky women' – she was being dragged off to be a white slave in the Middle-East.

The version with the castrated boy may have arisen from an earlier generations prejudice against Jewish communities.

The popularity and worldwide dispersal of urban legends involving crime and criminals is easy to imagine. Newspapers in North Wales, Leinster, Shropshire and Plymouth have published denials that child-snatchers are operating in shop toilets in their area. Each story contains a warning about a criminal practice, or the consequence of one moment of a lowered guard.

17

LONDON BLADES

A Whitechapel Beau: one who dresses with a
needle and thread and undresses with a knife.

◆

Attribute

✧ Hidden Blades ✧

Back in September 2010 I took part in an artist's workshop
on myth making. I took along a clipping about the dangers of
hidden razor blades to illustrate a London version of a popular
myth. Two of the group of eight said, 'Oh, you mean like the
hidden razor blades in the water slide at Crystal Palace swimming pool?' They were more than happy to join in this violent
idea of child-slicing with a broader tradition and share their stories. I came away with an addition to an urban myth and the
thought that this sort of thing is probably quite normal for an

artist's workshop on myth making, taking place in an abandoned shop at the top of the Elephant and Castle shopping centre.

In his book *Urban Legends Uncovered* Mark Barber told the same rumour about a nearby waterslide in Walton-on-Thames, Surrey. A Surrey chap himself, Barber told of a popular slide called 'The Black Hole' that children slid down in complete darkness. In 1985 a rumour persisted that 'gangs of youths' were stopping halfway down the slide and planting razorblades stuck down with chewing gum (for an extra unhygienic twist). A 13-year-old girl received serious injuries on her back and legs from using the slide. The popularity of 'The Black Hole' declined, and after a while the park, Barber reports, closed down.

A friend who grew up in south-west London remembered the same rumours being attached to a waterslide in Richmond. Again, it was chewing gum that held the blades in place. A strange message on an email list dedicated to lidos claimed that the 'Wild Waters' flume in Richmond Park was closed due to hidden blades injuring sliders and that a ghost known as 'The Phantom Slider of Richmond' haunted it, describing it as 'the most famous flume haunting in the UK'. I am not sure how serious the message on the lido list is. It does pick up the razor-hysteria which has spread far enough across the world that in America, where this legend is repeated, it is told that waterslides in England are banned because they bristled with hidden blades. American readers: this is not true.

In 2008, a 16-year-old worker in a McDonald's in New Plymouth, New Zealand, was cut by a broken pen whilst cleaning a children's play tunnel. The hidden-blade myth was well known enough that the blame was first put on a razor hidden there by persons unknown and with malicious intent to wound a child.

There's a similarity here to the ubiquitous urban legend of the razor blade hidden in the Halloween apple given to the trick or treating child. This legend transcends location, but is more popular in America. However, I've heard this repeated throughout my life, especially growing up during the 1970s and '80s. In his column 'Halloween Sadists', reprinted in *Curses! Broiled Again!*, Jan Harold Brunvand looked up the evidence for children being injured as a result of razor blades, syringes and poison hidden in their Halloween booty, and found none at all.

◇ **Cut by Tart Cards** ◇

It's not only children who are in danger of getting hurt when out enjoying themselves. There are urban myths of bloody razor blades hidden in the coin return of vending machines and syringes hidden in cinema seats and variations of both. When two women were attacked at a bus stop in Haringey – one on 18 November 2011 and the other on 23 November – by a man with a needle, their first fear was that they had contracted HIV from the assault. At the time of writing neither the attacker has been caught nor has the women's diagnosis, as far as I can find, been made public.

This leads to the story I told the artists in the Elephant and Castle shopping centre. I have a clipping from the now-defunct *London Lite* newspaper of a police warning issued in north London, of razor blades hidden behind prostitute cards in King's Cross and Euston. The also defunct *News of the World* printed similar stories of cards with blades in Westminster. 'Tart cards', as they are known, are a familiar part of the central London land-scape, and range from a quick description of the prostitute or specific services available written on a blank card in felt-tip to, thanks to cheap digital printing, full colour erotic images and a phone number. I've heard a rumour that one can track changes in the cards in different parts of London: regular sex in the West End and around the train stations, bondage and domination in the legal quarter of Lincolns Inn and things getting kinkier the further into the City of London one goes, the story being that the more affluent and high-powered one is, the more perverted one becomes.

The warning about the 'sex card booby trap' came from PC Dylan Belt of Camden Police. Gangsters were protecting their 'corner of the lucrative sex trade' by hiding traps behind their cards to prevent cleaners and rival gangs from removing them, and members of the public who may be interested in taking a card or two were warned against it. PC Belt is quoted as saying: 'We send the cleaners in and they find cards that have been booby-trapped. It could be with razor blades and they also use an irritant which burns the skin.'

An unnamed spokesman for British Telecom said, 'We will do everything we can to protect people using phone boxes,' which is what you would expect a spokesman to say whatever the danger.

There's a temptation here to read a broader narrative within this phenomenon. The forbidden fruit of the apple comes at us all the way from Genesis to Snow White to anonymous villains punishing children for their greed at Halloween and accepting gifts from strangers. I think it is worth noting that in almost every instance of scarring waterslides, HIV-laced syringes and maiming tart cards the victim is not doing something entirely virtuous. They are not all procuring prostitutes, but they are all engaged in something fun, even the innocent use of a vending machine or waterslide. Leisure, it seems, and particularly when it involves sliding down a wet surface or an enthusiastic bite into an ill-gotten apple, has its dangers. In the stiffly moral world of urban myths no one is ever harmed after committing a selfless act.

✧ The Chelsea Smilers and Friends ✧

Another urban myth that flourished in the 1980s in south London was that of the 'Chelsea Smilers'. The Smilers were a group of Chelsea football fans travelling London in a van with a smiley face painted on the side. They would stop schoolchildren and ask them questions about Chelsea football club. If the children got the questions wrong – perhaps they didn't support Chelsea or, worse, didn't like football – the gang would slice the corners of their mouth. They would then hit the child hard enough to make them scream, which would widen their wounds into a 'smile'. The thug's weapon of choice was a razor blade, knife or the edge of a credit card or phone card. Salt or vinegar was put onto the wounds to make the pain worse. A story of the Smilers' brutality always ended with a warning: the Chelsea Smilers were at another school yesterday, but they were coming to the child's school today.

In his book *London Lore*, Steve Roud talks about his daughter hearing the story in her school in Croydon in January and February 1989 and, from talking to her and her cousins at other schools, finding the myth at those other schools. By doing this, Roud was able to document the scare story as it spread: 'Many younger ones were in tears, some in hysterics, many refused to come home till their parents came to get them,' Steve writes. 'The children talked of nothing else.'

Roud was able to trace the rumour to where it began in Bexley, around 31 January 1989. It spread across south London, reaching Wandsworth, Merton and Sutton by the first week in March. Soon afterward, the story hit Kent and Surrey. He reported that the panic died down quickly, but the story became a standard playground scare story.

The phantom razor hiders and Chelsea Smilers are not the first imaginary gang to disfigure Londoners. 'The Mohawks', (also know as the Mohocks or Mowhawks) were a gang who wandered 1712 London. They were rumoured to have tattooed innocent faces, put fish hooks in people's cheeks and drag them along with a fishing line, and crush the noses, slit the ears and gouge out the eyes of their victims with 'new invented weapons'. The Mohawks were said to be like a horror-story version of the Bullingdon Club; rich young men who would meet in their clubs, drink to excess then head out, often into St James's Park, to cause havoc.

Another cruel trick of theirs was to put their sword between a man's legs and move it to make the poor chap dance, or to surround a man with their swords and one would stab him in his backside. The man would spin round to face his attacker and then another would stab him from behind. The idea was to keep the unfortunate fellow spinning around like a top.

With all of this cruelty on the street it may be surprising to learn there was was only one Mohawk trial. Sir Mark Cole and Viscount Hinchingbrooke are named in most books as the chief Mohawks. The total number of arrests was seven and the names read like a list of society party attendees: Edward Richard Montague, Lord Hinchingbroke; Sir Mark Cole, baronet; Thomas Fanshawe; Thomas Sydenham, gentleman; Captain John Reading; Captain Robert Beard; Robert Squibb of Lincoln's Inn, gentleman; and Hugh Jones, servant to Sir Mark Cole.

As recorded in *Chambers Book of Days* this aristocratic crew were put on trial for being 'mohocks'. Their crimes are explained below:

> … they had attacked the watch in Devereux Street, slit two persons' noses, cut a woman in the arm with a penknife so as to disable her for life, rolled a woman in a tub down Snow Hill, misused other women in a barbarous manner by setting them on their heads, and overset several coaches and chairs with short clubs, loaded with lead at both ends, expressly made for the purpose.

The defendants claimed that they themselves were vigilante 'scourers' and were out looking for Mohawks. After raiding and wrecking an illegal gambling den, the team heard that the Mohawks were in Devereux Street. On arrival they helped three wounded men, but the nightwatchman John Bouch, an early type of policeman, mistook the rich crime-fighters for Mohawks, attacked them and arrested them.

The jury found them guilty and fined them each three shillings and four pence, which even for the early eighteenth century seems quite cheap for a sadistic night out. It is not clear whether their victims were ever found or if they were invented by the nightwatch, and it doesn't prove much other than a group of privileged men were convicted for a night's misconduct. It does not prove that a conspiracy of Mohawks ever existed. With a lot of rumour and little evidence, the doubts about these stories grew. Jonathan Swift thought the Mohawks were the result of mass hysteria, and Daniel Defoe thought they had the 'air of Grub Street' about them: Grub Street being the home of London's cheaper and more sensationalist publishing and writers at the time – an earlier Fleet Street, if you will.

✧ Dashing Blades ✧

After the Mohawk moral panic of 1712 came the appearance of Spring-heeled Jack in 1838. Jack was a dark, iron-clawed, fire-breathing figure who would terrify people, often women, walking at night in London before making his getaway by leaping or bouncing over a wall with the aid of his spring-heeled boots. Jack is now thought of as a ghost or demon, some elemental presence spreading fear across London. He has featured in popular culture several times, from penny dreadfuls to comics to the fiction of Philip Pullman, as a supernatural or super-gadget bearing superhero.

The earliest description of Jack appeared in a letter from a Peckham resident to the Lord Mayor of London, published in *The Times* dated 9 January 1838, describing a dangerous bet laid by an affluent group of men:

> The wager has, however, been accepted, and the unmanly vil-
> lain has succeeded in depriving seven ladies of their senses,
> two of whom are not likely to recover, but to become burdens
> to their families. At one house the man rang the bell, and on the
> servant coming to open the door, this worse than brute stood
> in no less dreadful figure than a spectre clad most perfectly. The
> consequence was that the poor girl immediately swooned, and
> has never from that moment been in her senses. The affair has
> now been going on for some time, and, strange to say, the papers
> are still silent on the subject.

To do this, the 'unmanly villain' appeared in villages around London (including Peckham) disguised as 'a ghost, a bear and a devil', and had already left one woman so afraid she could not bear the sight of men. The Peckham resident thought that news or warning of this campaign had not yet appeared in the papers because those involved, being of higher ranks, had sought to keep the stories out of the press. In 1907, Jack was identified as the Marquess of Waterford, an aristocrat with a reputation for cruelty and practical jokes who would hide in dark places in costume, waiting to frighten people.

The identification with the rich may be twofold: firstly there is the idea that those in the higher echelons of society may have contempt for ordinary people and that they gain sport from tormenting and terrorising them. There is also the lack of capture or publicity about the great danger of Spring-heeled Jack. No Mohawk or Spring-heeled villain has ever been captured and shown to the public. This may be because they do not really exist and so are impossible to capture, but those convinced of their reality had other ideas: the Mohawks and Jack are rich and privileged and so escape arrest and publicity through their power.

The reality may be stranger and more sophisticated. Guising was popular in the seventeenth and eighteenth centuries, and dressing up as a ghost and walking the night, looking to frighten people was an almost common adult pastime. As well as Jack there was the Peckham ghost, Plumstead ghost and others. Mike Dash, in his authoritative *Spring-heeled Jack: To Victorian Bugaboo from Suburban Ghost*, investigated news reports on one of the most famous Spring-heeled Jack cases. As reported in *The Times* on 22 February 1838, Jane Alsop of Bearbinder Lane, Old Ford, answered a late-night ring at the door. She answered and the man at the door said, 'For God's sake, bring me a light, for we have caught Spring-heeled Jack in the lane.' Jane gave the candle to the man, who she thought was a policeman, but instead of running off with it he threw off his heavy cloak, put the candle to his chest and 'vomited forth a quantity of blue and white flames from his mouth'. Jane saw that the man was wearing a large helmet and that his clothes fitted him very tightly, like a white oilskin. Spring-heeled Jack, as the man was thought to be, darted toward her, catching her by the dress and back of her neck and placed her head under his arm. He began to tear at her dress with his claws and Jane screamed loudly for help. One of her sisters arrived and rescued her.

This account is the heart of the Spring-heeled Jack myth, and the description of the helmet and tight-fitting suit lead researchers in the 1970s to suggest that Jack was an alien running amok in early Victorian London. Mike Dash looked into supplementary accounts of the attack that covered the two investigations the newly formed Metropolitan Police opened to look into it. After a number of interviews, officers Young and Lea concluded that, 'In her fright the young lady had much mistaken the appearance of her assailant.' Two men, a bricklayer named Payne and a carpenter called Millbank, were seen walking away from Jane Alsop's house just after the attack. Millbank was wearing a white hat and a white fustian (heavy woven cloth shooting jacket), which the police thought was Jack's white oilskin. During the investigation, one James Smith, a wheelwright, described an encounter with Millbank and Payne later that evening on the Coborn Road. Millbank, the one in the shooting jacket, pulled the wheel Smith was carrying on his shoulder, and asked him, 'What have you got today to Spring Jack?' Smith replied that he desired Jack to give his wheel back. Smith told the police: 'I have no doubt but that the man Millbank was the person who so frightened the Misses Alsop.'

The myth of Spring-heeled Jack is of a lone monster, either man or a supernatural entity, scaring and assaulting the people of London. One big part of the myth is that it may have been an insane aristocrat. In a talk at the London Ghosts conference of October 2012, Mike Dash suggested that while the main suspect, the Marquess of Waterford, was known to have dressed in a devil costume at a party, this does not mean countless others were doing the same. It seems sensible to suggest that there was not one individual Spring-heeled Jack; this ghost, bear or devil was either a viral idea taken on by many men or something they did – guising in the city – that gained the label of Jack. Some may have been playing practical jokes, others have a more aggressive air to them, and many may have a blend of both.

✧ Saucy Jack ✧

If Spring-heeled Jack, the Chelsea Smilers and the Mohawks are moral panics, is it possible that another series of actual violent acts have a fictional boogieman attached to them? Is the Jack the Ripper mystery not a mystery at all but a moral panic grown into urban legend and conspiracy theory? I think parallels between the rumours of Mohawks and Spring-heeled Jack and the theories about Jack the Ripper are worth drawing.

That the murders themselves took place is not in doubt; that there was one killer, the enigmatic Jack in his cape and top hat carrying a surgeon's leather bag, is an unproven idea that has developed into a cultural icon. Historian Jan Bondeson wonders in an article in 'History Today' whether the moral panic over the prostitute murders in 1888 created a myth of a single killer. He reports that ripperologists disagree on the number of victims that Jack took, and that two may have been murdered by partners or ex-partners. The violent death of Polly Nichols, Jack the Ripper's first victim, caused a moral outrage, like his Spring-heeled forebear and the Mohawks, and a number of other deaths – Emma Smith, Martha Turner and Rose Mylett – were, at first, also attributed to Jack the Ripper. These deaths have not made it into the 'canonical five' murders for which most ripperologists think Jack the Ripper was responsible; Mary Ann Nichols, Annie Chapman, Elizabeth Stride, Catherine Eddowes and Mary Jane Kelly. Annie Millwood, Ada Wilson and Annie Farmer were all suggested Jack the Ripper victims or survivors, but have since been discounted from the ripper-orthodoxy. Another victim, the aptly named 'Fairy Fey', was allegedly found on 26 December 1887, 'after a stake had been thrust through her abdomen', but there are no records of a murder in Whitechapel over the Christmas period of 1887.

The authorities were unsure whether Rose Myatt had been murdered at all or whether she had choked to death whilst drunk. Writing about the death, Robert Anderson, the officer in charge of the investigation, thought if there had not been a Ripper scare, no one would have thought she had been murdered.

With the mythology of the Ripper has grown the idea that the killer has never been brought to light because of a conspiracy amongst the powerful. Leonard Matters, described by Alan Moore as 'the first ripperologist', in his appendix to *From Hell: the Dance of the Gull Catchers*, named a Dr Stanley as the Ripper in his book *The Mystery of Jack the Ripper*, published in 1929.

Stanley – not his real name – murdered and mutilated London prostitutes in revenge for his son's death from syphilis before fleeing to Argentina. Dr Stanley was no ordinary doctor, having a large aristocratic practice which no doubt protected him.

Prince Albert Victor, the grandson of Queen Victoria, was named as a possible Ripper suspect in the 1960s, after he was driven mad and angry as a result of catching syphilis from a prostitute. This rumour has evolved into the idea, popularised in Alan Moore's graphic novel and the film it inspired, that the Ripper was Sir William Gull, surgeon to Queen Victoria and a Freemason, another secretive group seen by some to be above the law. The conspiracy now is that Albert Victor had an affair with a woman which the Ripper victims found out about and were murdered by an insane Gull to cover up the truth.

Other suspects include the Duke of Clarence, Sir John Williams, who was obstetrician to Queen Victoria's daughter Princess Beatrice, and sensitive, creative types such as Lewis Carroll and painter Walter Sickert. Each suspect appears in a new book and with the continued growth in popularity of Ripper lore and the deepening of the myth, new and even more unlikely suspects are investigated all the time. After a long look comparing Jack the Ripper crime scene photographs and the paintings of Vincent van Gogh, writer Dale Larner has concluded that van Gogh was, indeed, Jack the Ripper. John Morris takes the idea of Sir John Williams being the Ripper, driven to insanity after not being able to have children, and transfers the crimes to his wife, Lizzie Williams, in his book *Jack the Ripper: The Hand of a Woman*. Bram Stoker, author of *Dracula* has never been in the frame for being Jack the Ripper, but The History Press book *The Dracula Secrets: Jack the Ripper and the Darkest Sources of Bram Stoker*, suggests that Jack the Ripper was, sort-of in a round-about-way, Dracula. That through 'a secret code' found in 'previously unpublished letters', Stoker wove details of Ripper suspect Francis Tumblety into his novel. This 'ripper code' was inspired by Stoker's relationship with Sir Thomas Hall Caine, to whom he dedicated *Dracula*. Caine also had a relationship with Tumblety, and Tumblety was fingered as a Ripper suspect in the book *Jack the Ripper: First American Serial Killer*. Tumblety was arrested in 1888 for 'gross indecency', and was possibly gay. Did this drive him to murder and mutilate women? I must confess that I have not read any of the above books; these theories are taken from promotional websites, press releases and news reports, so I have no idea whether each author is sincere, cynically milking the myth for money or undertaking a conceptual exercise in how evidence can be bent into the strangest proofs.

As well as Jan Bondeson, in 1986 Peter Turnbull published his book *The Killer Who Never Was*, putting forward the no-Ripper hypothesis. Ripperologist and tour guide John G. Bennett published *Jack the Ripper: The Making of the Myth* in 2011 which, while not denying the single-killer hypothesis, did much to disembowel the countless scabbed-over theories about the original murders. Retired murder-squad detective Trevor Marriott brought his experience into investigating the Jack the Ripper killings and concluded that there was no Jack. If the evocative name Jack the Ripper had not been attached to the Whitechapel killings, the theory would have been forgotten a long time ago. He decided that at least two of the women 'were killed by the same hand' and the others, if they were related at all, were copycat killings. 'The urban myth was created by an overzealous newspaper reporter sending a mysterious letter signed Jack the Ripper. The police certainly never believed in a killer known as Jack the Ripper.'

These theories are a little way from the Mohawks' dangerous rakes, but nearer the fantastical attacks of Spring-heeled Jack. It is the idea of a rich and debauched individual committing murder and mutilation and escaping justice because of their privilege, that all of these blade-wielding figures, fact or fiction, share. The actual, certain evidence for the Whitechapel killings is the bodies of the victims. The theories and the name Jack the Ripper came in the hysteria afterwards, a hysteria that still bends thought. There may have been one murderer, or each killing could have had its own sad story, but the idea of a Victorian killer named Jack the Ripper has such gravity to it that people cannot resist its pull.

18 THE ACCIDENTAL THEFT

Our old cat died last night
Me wife says to bury it out of sight
But we didn't have a garden;
We was livin' in a flat
So what was I to do with the body of a cat,
Then a big brown paper bag I spied
I put our old dead kittycat inside.
And now I'm off down the street with the body in the bag,
The body in the bag, ta ra ra.

♦

'The Body in the Bag' by Charles O'Hegarty

JAN HAROLD BRUNVAND often mutters in his books that one should 'never trust a dead cat story'. So consider yourself warned while I tell you the tale of the single 'lady scholar' working at the British Museum who fended off loneliness by sharing her lodgings with a cat. This is a story Brunvand collected for his 1983 book *The Vanishing Hitchhiker*, which may be why a 'lady scholar' isn't just a scholar. She smuggled the cat into her room, bribed the maid to keep quiet and lived with the cat over winter. In time, though, the cat died and with no garden in which to bury the cat, our scholar neatly and secretly parcelled the cat up to put into the building's incinerator. She was interrupted by the establishment's proprietor and thought, 'this will never do', and so headed off to the British Library. (This would have been when the library was within the British Museum.) She saw a good place along the way to get rid of the cat – a culvert – but this time a policeman came round the corner just when she was about to do the deed.

Some days you just can't get rid of a dead cat, so she took the parcel to the museum and, at lunchtime, was stopped by the guard letting her know that she had forgotten her package. 'This is getting funny,' she thought to herself. She had failed to leave her dead pet on the bus and on the tube, so in desperation rang her friend who told her to come to her, as there was a local pet cemetery in which she could inter the cat.

When she arrived, perhaps filled with guilt at the way she had tried to abandon the cat's remains, she opened the parcel to have one last look at the cat and found … a leg of mutton.

The first part of this legend makes it into Mark Barber's book *Urban Legends Uncovered*, albeit in a dishevelled state, with a 'young lady' who worked at the British Museum living in a one-bedroom flat with her beloved cat. Not wanting to bin it and with nowhere to bury the cat she set out to inter it in the nearest pet cemetery, which was 10 miles away. She put the cat in a box and the box into a large carrier bag. On the way to this distant animal graveyard she popped into a clothes shop that she did not visit very often, due to it being so far out of central London. While in the shop and looking at a couple of dresses, she put her bag down for a second and when she reached for it again, the bag was gone.

Then there was a disturbance outside the shop: a woman had fainted on the street. Our bereaved cat owner saw that the unconscious woman had her missing bag clutched to her chest, with the head of her dead cat poking out of the top of it. The passed-out woman was a known shoplifter who had been operating in the area for months.

This second version of the dead cat story is as classic an urban myth as babies in microwaves and hairy handed hitchhikers. Its purpose is clear as a revenge fantasy for those who have been robbed, and versions of it appear all over the western world. Whilst dead cats are very popular, often it is a bag of collected dog excrement that is snatched in a park, or a urine sample in a whisky bottle stolen by a thirsty thief. It is a stray old alley cat of a story that crops up, occasionally mangy and reeking, to the party. It is easy to understand the ubiquity of this story, as everyone wishes ill on the person who has snatched their bag or picked their pocket. Some years ago my wife had her bag snatched on Whitechapel High Street while on the way home from a gig. She had been to her dance class before that and the bag contained only her worn dance kit. A few days later, a friend imagined the thief getting back to his crime den with nothing but a used women's dance outfit and his boss making him wear the worthless costume and dance on a table for him as a punishment.

Managing to swap a dead cat for a tasty piece of dead sheep is a different outcome, and has the cat-carrier inadvertently becoming the thief themselves. The constant attempts to dispose of the package end with something far more valuable than a departed pet for one and, presumably, a frustrated roast dinner elsewhere in London for the other.

The mistaken theft crops up a lot in British folklore. A chestnut of a tale that is as common as the dead cat tale is the story of the valuable thing left on the mantelpiece (not the most inspiring title for an urban myth, but please bear with me).

One version of this tale starts with Peter, who is on a business trip in London, discovering that his gold watch is missing while he is travelling back to his hotel on the last tube train.

On the platform is a young man grinning at him and Peter decides that this man must be the thief. He leaps up from his seat and grabs the young man by the lapels of his suit, only for the tube doors to close in front of him, tearing the man's suit lapels off.

Back at his hotel room Peter phones the police to report the theft and then phones his wife to let her know his gold watch is gone. His wife says, 'I'm glad you rang. Did you know you'd left your watch behind on the dresser this morning?'

Other versions have the 'robbed' man wrestling his wallet from the thief, only to find it at home, or the more genteel version with an elderly lady going into town by train with £5. She dozes off during the journey and when she wakes, there is another sleeping woman in the carriage. She then goes into her bag to check her shopping list, finds her £5 is missing and, on impulse, checks the bag of the sleeping woman. There, at the top of the bag, is the £5 note. She removes it quietly and decides not to confront the woman or report her, so leaves her sleeping in the train compartment. With her shopping done, her husband meets her at the station and asks, 'However did you get all that stuff? You left your £5 note on the mantelpiece.'

Both dead cat stories, the accidental theft and the bag-snatcher, are intertwined. In another version the dead cat is taken while the woman has lunch with a friend. The thief faints in the toilets whilst checking her ill-gotten gains and the cat owner finds the theft and the cat package she was trying to lose. As the thief is stretchered away the woman passes the repackaged cat to the paramedics with the words, 'I think this is hers.'

The trope of wandering London looking for a place to leave a dead cat because you do not have a garden is older than this urban legend. It was recalled by Eric Winter in a musical song he recorded in the journal *Sing* on 5 July 1960. The song 'The

Body in the Bag' by Charles O'Hegarty is a cockney music-hall song about a frustrated man who is trying to leave a cat somewhere. The lyrics mirror the troubles of our British Museum lady scholar:

> I went off down the street to have a whisky neat
> And carefully laid my dead cat underneath my seat.
> Then I got down on my hands and knees;
> Went halfway through the town,
> When the barman stops me,
> 'Here's your parcel Mr. Brown,'
> So I had to thank the silly fool
> And give him half a crown
> For bringing me the body in the bag.

Having failed all day to get rid of the cat, Mr Brown hears a noise in the bag:

> All at once from in the bag
> There came a plaintive meow
> Say Puss, 'I'm dead no longer,
> You needn't bother now.
> You've often heard it said
> That a cat has got nine lives,
> Well, I'm a married Tabby,
> One of Tommy's wives
> And our families they usually come
> In threes, and fours, and fives.'
> But there were seven little bodies in the bag!

Another accidental theft is the urban legend about two travellers and a packet of biscuits. Printed versions appeared around 1972/74 and the legends appeared in Folklore from the summer of 1975. A traveller buys a cup of tea and a packet of biscuits in a Joe Lyons corner house, opposite Liverpool Street station (or in a buffet car or station café), and sits down to enjoy them. Also sitting at the table is an African (or Pakistani or West Indian) man, who helps himself to one of the biscuits. Shaken by the effrontery of this, our traveller takes another. The uninvited biscuit-eater takes another and this continues until they are down to the last biscuit. Here the African (West Indian or Pakistani) man breaks the biscuit in two and hands the traveller half. Our traveller loses his temper at this point and hurls abuse at the man. It is only then that he (or sometimes she) realises that his own packet of biscuits is lying unopened on his suitcase, and that he had been helping himself to the other fellow's biscuits.

This story made it as far as Paul Smith's *The Book of Nastier Legends* published in 1986, where the setting was a café in Southampton, biscuits became the fingers of a Kit-Kat bar and the patient and sharing individual changed from an ethnic minority and possible recent immigrant to an 'outrageously dressed' punk. The message of the story is the same as with the tea house: don't judge people by how they look and, as with all of these stories, double check before confronting someone and do not be so suspicious. Also, take better care of your cat, be it dead or alive.

CONCRETE JUNGLE

*If you took the city of Tokyo and turned it upside down and
shook it you would be amazed at the animals that would fall out.
It would pour more than cats and dogs, I tell you.*

✦

Yann Martel, Life of PI

✧ Rat Land ✧

In London you are never more than a certain distance away from
a rat. This is an almost universal indicator of urban filth, London's
hidden dangers and the fear and loathing a lot of us have for rats.
Each time the idea of rat proximity is repeated the distance varies.
A quick Google suggests 6ft, 7ft, 10ft or a metric 5m or 18m.
Why do we even think it's possible to have an average distance
from a rat? Do London rats outnumber London human beings?
This idea seems to come from the 1909 book *The Rat Problem*
by W.R. Boelter who undertook his research by asking country

folk whether they thought it was reasonable to say that there was one rat per acre of land. Boelter made an estimated guess at 40 million rats, as there were 40 million acres of cultivated land in Britain at the time. There were also around 40 million people in Britain at the time. Since then, it only seems right to think that the rat population has increased more quickly than the human population, rats must breed like rats after all, and so now they must outnumber us, particularly in our grimy cities.

Luckily, Dr Dave Cowan, leader of the wildlife programme at the Food and Environment Research Agency, has tried to work out the actual person:rat ratio of Britain – both town and country – in a more scientific way. Counting cities, sewers and farms (farms are the most popular rat territories), Dr Cowan calculated that there are 10.2 million rats in Britain. The UK has 60 million human inhabitants, so people outnumber rats by six to one. As for approximate distance from a rat in an urban area you would be, at most, never more than 164ft (50m) away from a rat. Although you may, of course, be much nearer.

✧ Parakeet Superstars ✧

Unlike the pigs living in London's sewers or the big cats roaming its suburbs, the parakeets of London are not an urban legend in themselves. They have been reported across London, from Twickenham to Boreham Wood to Hither Green. My own visits to open spaces in London, from Kensal Green cemetery to Manor House Gardens in Lee, have been cut through by a flash of green and a sharp parakeet squawk. Ring-necked parakeets cover south and west London, while the Monk Parakeet has colonies in north London. One encounter with the ring-necked variety in February 2011 in Richmond Park was like a Mardi Gras version of Alfred Hitchcock's *The Birds*; the old oak trees were thick with their bright feathers and delirious parakeet chatter.

How they arrived in London is another story, or rather stories. I first encountered the legend of west London's parakeets in a copy of *Time Out* from June 2005, which claimed they are all descended from a pair that escaped from Jimi Hendrix's flat in Notting Hill. The two birds were like the guitarist himself: exotic and flamboyant in a cold grey London. On escaping, they went to found a nation of parakeets in London and provide a high-pitched, alien soundtrack to the coo of London's pigeons and chattering of sparrows. In a south London special of the *Evening Standard*'s *ES Magazine* in 2012, the parakeets were released by Hendrix, rather than escaping, and *Surrey Life* magazine in December 2011 imagined Hendrix playing 'Little Wing' as they sailed from the window and into Notting Hill.

In its 'Myth Busters' column, the *Fortean Times*, in January 2010, describes a version that is just that little bit more dramatic, as the parakeets are accidentally released from Hendrix's flat following his death. From medieval to Victorian art, the human soul can be depicted as a dove departing through the window at the moment of death. Perhaps Hendrix's soul couldn't be anything as tame as a single, cooing dove.

Another story tells of the parakeets being the descendants of film stars rather than the pets of a pop star. The same *Time Out* article repeated the story that the parakeets are descended from some birds that escaped Shepperton Studios during the filming of the 1951 film *The African Queen*. A friend offered me another version in 2012, by suggesting the parakeets were related to a different African queen, having flown from the set of the 1963 film *Antony and Cleopatra*.

Yet another account describes a mass escape during the great storm of 1987, when an aviary was damaged in Northdown Park in Kent. If that is not dramatic enough, how about the parakeets being freed from quarantine at Heathrow airport by a storm? Or that a plane fuselage crashed landed on an aviary near Heathrow airport, or that the birds flew to freedom when the tanker that carried them ran aground or capsized? In many urban myths the parakeets of London do not arrive gradually; the story has to be 'disaster!' followed by an 'instant parakeet hoard!'

Another celebrity version of the parakeet origin myth is that they were escapees from the aviaries of King Manuel II, Manuel the Unfortunate (the Portuguese king who ascended to the throne after the assassination of his father and brother and had to flee on 6 October 1910 during Portugal's republican revolution). Manuel landed in Fulwell Park, Twickenham, for his exile where, it has been said, he attempted to recreate Portuguese life, including building an insecure cage for some parakeets. I have not been able to discover whether this story pre-dates the Hendrix one or if they are related. In any case, the parakeets are in London and any slightly exotic figure could be linked to their origins.

The story of the parakeets escaping Shepperton Studios is undone a little when it is pointed out that *The African Queen* was not filmed there but at Isleworth Studios. Isleworth may be quite near to Shepperton (as the parakeet flies), but no parakeets were imported for the making of the film. Britain has had a long history with these birds. In its factsheet on feral parakeets, the Department for Environment, Food and Rural Affairs states: 'There is a long history of occurrence in GB, with a first record of breeding in Norfolk in 1855. However the present naturalised population dates only from 1969.'

A 1999 census of parakeets, which includes London, describes the birds as 'successfully breeding in the wild in the south east of England since 1969', suggesting there may be a Hendrix link (Hendrix died in 1970). It depends on how long it took the parakeets to get productive before anyone noticed. The census describes the origin of the birds as numerous escapes leading to 'many feral populations'. Although it is a great story to imagine that one famous parakeet owner is the daddy to the birds all around us, there are, of course, hundreds of anonymous parakeet owners who may have lost or released their pets.

The book *Parrots*, by Cyril H. Rogers, says of the Ring-necked parakeet that they are 'probably the most common of all the "Polly Parrots"', so it is perhaps no surprise that enough have escaped to form a breeding population across south London. And no matter how virile the parakeets of Jimi Hendrix may have been, they surely haven't populated all of London with birds.

That all of these stories involve an accident having such a sudden effect on our environment, like a clumsy rock legend, an aviary smashed in an historic storm or a tanker running aground, says a lot more about the human need for narrative than it does about Anglo-Indian parakeets. The numbers and visibility of this relatively new arrival must, it seems, indicate that they come from one event or source: a disaster, an exotic recreation of Africa on a film set, or a rock star opening up his window and sending out bright-coloured birds across the city. The banal explanation of cage and aviary escapees, with long lifespans and fruitful breeding cycles, adapting to our environment does not satisfy.

An article from *ES Magazine* in 2012 on cosmopolitan south London described the parakeets as 'cheeky birds' and as a 'cheery sight in parks from Greenwich to Brixton to Richmond', while the book *Fauna Britannica* has the Spickett family of Twickenham describing them as 'invading Benfleet more than thirty years ago' and records their glee at a pair being mobbed out of a spruce tree by the local magpies. *The Times*, perhaps with its tongue in its cheek, fears that the parakeets are almost a harbinger of environmental and immigration doom. The parakeets are 'the latest, and loudest, evidence of global warming' as well as '[…] further disquieting proofs of shifts in the natural world: ornithologists fear that these parakeets – robust, adaptable and aggressive – will impinge on the habitat of indigenous species such as starlings, kestrels and little owls.'

Fear not for our little owls just yet though. The RSPB's policy on parakeets, last updated in 2009, does not offer any evidence that parakeets are a threat to other species, nor does a 2011 article published in *Ibis: The International Journal of Avian Science*. Others differ, and in 2011, DEFRA instigated a cull of Monk Parakeets to stop the £1.7 billion-a-year damage they allegedly cause to the British economy.

These out-of-place, bright birds couldn't have as mundane an origin as London's iconic pigeons, which are also feral animals with similar origins. The rock pigeon's native environment is the western coast of Britain. Our London version is descended from domesticated rock doves that have escaped their coops and turned feral on London's streets, buildings and parks. They have been in London for a long time; so long, in fact, that they are very much a part of London's landscape. Fourteenth-century Londoners threw so many stones at pigeons that they would break the windows of St Paul's, and Pepys pitied them during the Great Fire of London. They have been with us so long they no longer need a story to explain their presence, unlike the parakeet.

Parakeets have appeared in the UK under much stranger circumstances than being celebrity escapees: in 1895, *The Field* magazine reported a parakeet sighting in a farmyard in Gledfield, Scotland, two years after another parakeet had visited. No one local had claimed to have lost a parakeet.

⬦ Crack Squirrels and Squirrats ⬦

If the poor rat and feral parakeet are abused for the purpose of demonstrating the corrupting effects city living has on nature, then please pity the poor grey squirrels. Dubbed and damned as 'tree rats' for their bird-table raiding ways and being a large immigrant from America that has driven the indigenous red squirrel to the far corners of the kingdom, in summer 2007 the *Sun* newspaper accused them of a much closer relationship with London's rats. On 31 July it published a photograph of a squirrel with a bare, rat-like tail, taken by central London artist Sia Sumaria.

The next day Tom Crew photographed a rat-tailed squirrel on his tree-lined road in Dulwich. Had squirrels and rats interbred to produce 'squirrats' – a fearless urban hybrid?

'The one I saw wasn't afraid of anything and seemed quite tame,' said Mr Crew. 'Most squirrels dart up a tree when you approach them, but this breed is very confident and stood its ground. I've seen a whole family of them in my road. The hairless tail makes them look so strange.'

Unnamed experts suggested that squirrels and rats cannot interbreed and instead of a cross-rodent love-in, the squirrats are simply squirrels with a diseased, bare tail.

Possibly not quite as bad as rutting with rats is the suggestion on the front page of the *South London Press* on 7 October 2005 that the grey squirrels of Brixton were crackheads. It quoted a local resident who 'did not wish to be named' who had seen an ill-looking squirrel with bloodshot eyes digging in his garden. An hour later, a neighbour informed him that local crack dealers and users had been using his front garden to hide their rocks of crack.

The rest is left to the reader's imagination. Such a weak story was still quirky enough to make the *Daily Mirror*, the *Guardian* and the squirrel-damning *Sun*. By 18 October, *Fox News* in the US were repeating the story of London's crack squirrels with a mention of a footnote in the *South London Press'* story that crack squirrels were already a problem in New York and Washington DC. Squirrels on crack even made it into the BBC adult puppet show about urban animals, *Mongrels*.

So, squirrels of London, please tell us straight, we don't need to know about the rat sex, but do you have a crack problem?

Researching the story for a *Fortean Times* article, Ben Austwick found a location for the original, unnamed source for the story. On 3 October 2005, a user on the Urban 75 South London web forum began a post that began by matching the report in the *South London Press*. The user posted about dealers and users hiding their stash and squirrels, which were not ill-looking or bloodshot-eyed, that had been digging in their garden, and then they joked about the squirrel mistaking a rock of crack for a nut or acorn: 'But what if they did? And do I face the prospect of dreaded crack squirrels? Turf wars (flower bed wars) between dealers and squirrels?'

A joke on an internet forum was picked up by a journalist on a local London newspaper who fitted it into a news story. This is why there is no positive sighting of a squirrel chewing on crack; the original poster did not describe it and the journalist chose not to invent that part. Perhaps that would have been too dishonest.

✧ The Spider in the Supermarket ✧

A popular urban legend from the 1980s, which is currently dormant, is the tale of the squeaking pot plant. It was brought home and, in one version, made squeaking noises when watered, which the woman plant owner thought was the sound of air escaping from the dried pot as the water went in. Then the earth began to shift around the base of the plant, and so she called the police. In turn, the police called the local zoo who removed a large female tarantula and her nest of fifty youngsters. In the London version the spider is discovered at Kew Gardens. Kew's plant inspector, Jim Kessing, said, 'One of our gardeners said it happened to a friend of his son's. He asked me if it was possible. I told him it was – but a bit unlikely.' Tom Kelly, the manager of the Marks & Spencer Oxford Circus branch, lamented in 1985 that 'it's getting beyond a joke. Now we've got an official complaint from the Irish Ministry of Agriculture because someone in Dublin claims one of our people offered a woman £100 to keep it quiet!' Was that in cash or M&S vouchers? This story was so popular that it made the cover of Paul Smith's *The Book of Nastier Legends* in 1986, passing from person to person in a crowded pub. On the record, Marks & Spencer denied the possibility of illegal immigrant spider families invading London hidden in pot plants, as the African yuccas were all replanted in the Netherlands before arriving in our supermarkets.

Baby spiders feature in another 1970s and '80s urban legend that addresses the danger of travel and foreign lands, with the tale of the girl being bitten while on holiday on the coast of North Africa, or being bitten while on the plane heading home to London. In a Glaswegian version the bites fester until the girl goes to wash her wound and, positioned in front of a mirror to gain maximum horror, her face erupts with baby spiders.

Whilst that story is thankfully not true, a similar legend of tarantulas lurking in supermarket bananas is something that really does happen. On 4 June 2013, Mark Drinkwater was shopping at a Lidl in Sydenham. He reached into a banana box and out came a large spider attached to a bunch of bananas. He told the *News Shopper* on 13 June:

> It was the size of the palm of my hand. It was hairy. It was scary enough. I shook the banana and the tarantula fell back into the box. It probably wasn't very happy having been thrown back in the box. At the time I didn't panic, I was relatively calm, but later I could feel my heart beating through my chest. I decided not to buy the bananas.

He informed Lidl staff that there was a possible tarantula in the box and there followed a fine piece of improvisation: staff located the largest Tupperware bowl they could find and trapped the beast. Mr Drinkwater was put off buying bananas for a few weeks.

I emailed Lidl press and public relations office, and PR Manager Clare Norman confirmed the story and continued it. The 'unidentified spider' (Clare's words) was contained in the shop's disposal freezer while the RSPCA was contacted. They suggested Lidl contact the British Arachnological Society, who advised the staff to keep the spider in the freezer 'for a length of time' until it could be 'subsequently disposed of'.

I had to double check what that meant and it turns out that the best way to deal with a tarantula, which is how the spider was referred to in my second email from Clare Norman, is to freeze it. The freezer was their animal by-products freezer, which presumably, is where all the remains from the butchers' counter go so they do not decay too unpleasantly until they can be disposed of properly. The animal by-products service provider took the contents of the freezer, tarantula and all, and incinerated it. Just in case I did feel sad for the tarantula, who was a long way from home, Clare did reassure me that during incineration 'the energy from it is then used for electricity and other renewable energies.' I now think of the spider whenever I switch on the kettle to make a cup of tea.

✧ Spontaneous Snakes ✧

A little-known fact about London is that it often sprouts spontaneous snakes. Rodney Dale, in *The Tumour in the Whale*, tells the tale of a man finding a sleeping snake while strolling through Regents Park. Presuming it had slithered out of nearby London Zoo, the snake keeper was called while other staff members watched over the serpent. Once captured and checked over, the snake was found not to be an escapee. More snakes were found: a London & North Western van driver found a boa constrictor in his van and the son of an MP found a huge snake in a room in his father's London house.

More recently, in 2002, the New Grapes Church band were returning from playing at a wedding in Westminster to their church on John Wilson Street in Woolwich, when they found a 6ft python in their van. The previous people that had hired the van had managed to leave their snake behind.

There was no such simple explanation for the snake recorded by Charles Fort in his 1931 book *Lo!* A snake appeared on Gower Street, Bloomsbury, in 1920 in the garden of a Dr Michie.

And what was the explanation for the rogue reptile? It was a *naja haje*, an Egyptian cobra, which, therefore, must have been kept by a foreign student staying on Gower Street: 'The oriental snake had escaped from an oriental student.' Fort saw through this though, stating: 'I don't see that oriental students having oriental snakes is any more likely than American students should have American snakes: but there is an association here that will impress some persons.'

◇ The Penguin Entertained ◇

A penguin popped out of a duffle bag when a boy sat down to his tea after a visit to the zoo. His mother telephoned the zoo, but after a count the zoo keepers found, like the snakes at London Zoo, that they had a full complement. There's a joke about a penguin; the earliest version I've found is in *The Tumour in the Whale*. A man walking up St John's Wood Road was approached by a penguin. The man found a policeman, asked him what to do with the bird, and was told, 'Take him to the zoo if I were you, Sir.' The next day the policeman saw man and penguin walking again. 'I thought I said you should take the penguin to the zoo,' the policeman said. 'I did,' replied the man, 'and this afternoon we're going to the pictures.'

There is something about a penguin abroad that appeals to people. It may just be down to them being cute yet awkward birds that walk about on two legs. How long had the penguin wandered north London before approaching the young man for a date at the zoo? People do steal penguins from zoos: in 2012 two drunk Welsh tourists stole Dirk the Penguin from Seaworld on Queensland's Gold Coast, and a penguin was taken from Dublin Zoo in summer 2010 and found wandering the streets a few hours later. The question to ask here is which came first, the urban myth or the penguin theft?

THE FANTASTIC URBAN FOX

✧ Urban Foxes Abound! ✧

There is a reversal to the trend of out-of-place animals invading London story, and that's urban animals invading the greener and more pleasant British countryside. So rather than an urban legend about London, these stories are about how London is seen in other parts of the United Kingdom. In October 2004 the conservative MP for Lichfield, Michael Fabricant, tabled a parliamentary question for the then environment secretary, Margaret Beckett, about the dumping of urban foxes. He had learned of this while visiting Snowdonia. 'With the growing problem of increasing numbers of foxes in our towns and cities, it seems that do-gooders are now transporting live urban foxes from the West Midlands and other conurbations and releasing them into rural Wales where it is thought they will do no harm,' said Fabricant in a 10 October 2004 press release (which is still on his website at the time of writing). 'Instead, they are savaging sheep, poultry, and pets in hill farming country.'

His views on foxes were backed by Nick Smyth of Llwyngwril near Dolgellau, in a letter to the *Dysynni and Cambrian News*:

> A van in a motorway car park was found by acquaintances of ours to be full of urban foxes. When questioned, the driver stated that the animals were being taken to a remote part of the country, where no one lived and no one, in London presumably, had ever heard of, where he said they would do no harm ...

Smyth goes on to say that worse still, 'the driver could not pronounce the name of our village.' Smyth reported that farmers had shot more foxes than usual in the past three months, having dispatched 118. 'Somehow the ignorance of these town-dwellers and misguided do-gooders has got to be dispelled,' Mr Smyth muttered.

The supposed ignorant townies and do-gooders were the real issue with these migrant foxes. Rumours of urban fox dumping began over ten years earlier with the Farmers Union of Wales (FUW) issuing a press release entitled 'RSPCA accused of Mass Fox Releases'. It claimed that a farmer helping a lorry out of a ditch discovered a strange cargo. It carried forty-seven urban foxes, which were being transported by the RSPCA from Birmingham to their new pastoral Welsh home. The foolishness of this was outlined by Kim Brake of the FUW as these 'townie' foxes have 'little hope of surviving; and [it is] unfair to farmers who have to pick up the bill in slaughtered lambs.'

Hunt supporters in Cumbria claimed their local fox population had suddenly doubled, and that the new foxes looked and acted differently to the indigenous Lakeland foxes. Ted Bland, a hunt supporter with Lunesdale Foxhounds in Lancashire, claimed to have seen four foxes released from a van, whilst other reports claimed that vans carrying seventy foxes and lorries with up to 200 were heading out of the cities and into farmland ready to unload what was presumably drugged urban foxes.

The stories continued. A broken-down lorry carried ninety-seven urban foxes into Wales, with the men being paid £5 per fox to get them out of the cities. In West Somerset a blue van with no number plates was sighted doing a night-time fox deposit. Possible London foxes were described in Tendring, Essex, as 'not even scared of headlights'. Henry Gibbon said, 'The other day one fox looked down the barrel of my gun as if to say good morning.' These were hardened urban foxes.

From the cities themselves came doubt and enquiry about these fox-ferrying stories. Wild fox welfare charity the Fox Project ridiculed them, and the League Against Cruel Sports investigated, contacting almost every animal shelter in the UK and making extensive enquiries with local authorities: all denied dumping foxes. The BBC's rural news and magazine programme *Countryfile* put its money where its mouth was by offering a £1,000 reward for information that led to the identification of any animal welfare groups involved in fox smuggling. Not a penny of licence fee money has been paid out.

Why were fox hunters and their followers getting angry about not-so-fresh foxes being delivered to their land to be hunted? The claim was that it swelled the local fox population to levels dangerous to other wildlife, with more hungry, city foxes spreading mange amongst the rural ones, and that the urban foxes, suddenly finding themselves in an unpolluted and open environment, were lost, confused and prone to a swift and painful demise. And not only by hunting dogs.

As John Bryant pointed out in his 'Hunters & Dumpers' article in Issue 73 of the *Fortean Times*, the 1994 fox-dumping rumours emerged at the same time as Labour MP William MacNamara's private Wild Animals (Protection) Bill was brought before the House of Commons. The bill sought to make law a six-month prison sentence for anyone inflicting unnecessary suffering on a wild animal, and ban the use of dogs to 'kill, injure, pursue or attack'. It was an attempt to outlaw hunting. This attempt failed, but in 2004, with the Smyth and Fabricant fox-myths fuming in the background, the Labour government passed the Hunting Act, making hunting live animals with dogs illegal.

✧ Urban Fox Hunts ✧

As wild foxes were supposedly saved from being hunted in the countryside, their lives in London became more dangerous. The first mention of an urban fox hunt I have found is from gonzo free-sheet *Vice* in December 2003. Kid A and Kid B of Lambeth were asked why they hunted foxes, aside from the financial gain. Apparently Lambeth council charged £200 to shoot a fox but the street youth 'only charge a tenner'. 'Fuck it, I'm street. They shit by the swings anyway,' said Kid A in a touching mixture of childlike indignation and lack of empathy. Their preferred method was to drug the foxes' food, wait until the poison affected them and then beat them to death with a bat, or shoot them with a pellet gun.

It's not all anger though; Kid A says, 'I wanna get a fox for a pet anyway. I want to track it back to its lair, get hold of a little cub fox, innit. Take it for walks. Train it to fight.'

Is it just a story? There is blurry photo of two boys on bikes, one with a fox over his shoulder, complete with black bars across their eyes. This would need to have been faked, but such things are not difficult with a stuffed fox prop.

BBC London radio DJ and London enthusiast Robert Elms heard the urban fox-hunt story and would occasionally disappear into a reverie of Mod fox hunting conjecture, cruising London in sharp suits on scooters looking for pesky, pestilent foxes to punish. I think radio has a big influence on the dissemination of urban myths; it's a human voice telling you a story or wondering about a curiosity that is heard by thousands of people. The content of a regular with unscripted and informal dialogue from the presenter and guests is an environment where myths can evolve, and the amount of content makes them difficult to catalogue and reference.

In August 2010, a video was released on YouTube by a group called the Urban Foxhunters, which shows them hunting down a drugged fox and killing it with a cricket bat. The group, claiming to be from around Victoria Park, hated foxes and saw killing them as a public service, describing it as 'a bit unpleasant but it has to be done to keep our streets safe. I have kids and I don't want them being bitten by a diseased vermin scum, what's wrong with that?'

One member, Lone Horseman, wrote on the blog: 'For the record – when we kill these foxes they are dosed up with Xanax, which if you haven't tried it is a trippy anti-anxiety drug. Trust me these fuckers are dying with a smile on their face.'

If this sounds like an absurd Chris Morris-style way of baiting the media, that is because it is. It echoes closely with *Vice*'s 2003 fox hunts in Lambeth, though this could be a coincidence from both parties thinking through the logistics of catching a fox in London. Shortly after, the story appeared right across the British press. Most were appalled by the bludgeoning of a wild animal, 'diseased vermin scum' or not. The Metropolitan Police's wildlife crime unit began to make enquiries, and both the Fox Project and John Bryant, who offers a 'humane deterrence' service for wild animals, each put forward a £1,000 reward for the identity of the group. Meanwhile in the *Evening Standard*, 'London Diary' columnist Sebastian Shakespeare made another fox-linked political point and enthused:

Those urban fox killers are a perfect (or imperfect) example of Cameron's Big Society in action.

Dave wants to empower communities to do things for themselves. People power, he calls it, redistributing power from the government to the man and woman on the street. 'These are the things you do because it's your passion,' says the PM. Well, you can't accuse the fox killers of lacking passion. There is no denying they are performing a public service. It is about time we learned to be big enough not to have small feelings about foxes. They are pests. And as we now know they have changed their habits and started attacking children.

The 'Big Society' was the plan to cover billions of pounds of cuts to local authorities for essential services by getting passionate volunteers to do them for free. So, while an expensive municipal government offers trained council workers removing foxes with snares and rifles, the Big Society produces a vigilante group with cricket bats and prescription drugs battering a poisoned wild animal to death.

It must be extremely exciting to watch your hoax take on its own life, particularly when it was designed to highlight the media. The urban fox hunting video was produced by film makers Chris Atkins and Johnny Howorth as a response to calls by newspapers and politicians to begin culling urban foxes. These calls were in response to an attack by a fox on nine-month-old twins, Isabella and Lola Koupparis, in their bedroom, near Victoria Park in Hackney. Angry about the attack, one blogger demanded 'Bring Back Fox Hunting Now', and the Labour government's ban on fox hunting was never far from people's thoughts when discussing the urban fox problem. Atkins and Howorth had already produced the film *Starsuckers*, which was another shot at British media in which they sold fake stories to newspapers about celebrities. They managed to get unverified and ridiculous stories published, including Guy Ritchie giving himself a black eye whilst drunkenly juggling with cutlery, and a friend of Amy Winehouse punching the late singer in the hair after Winehouse had accidently set it on fire. Both are very easy to check, even via a photograph, but still made it into the newspapers. A blog and Facebook group was set up for the urban fox hunters and a video was released, showing a fox being clubbed to death in Victoria Park. Once leaflets started to be distributed around Hackney seeking the 'hunters', and the death threats arrived online, Atkins and Howorth quickly owned up to the *Guardian* and released a making-of film of the original fox-hunting film, featuring the pair, some friends and a dog called Monty wrapped in fox fur. A stuffed fox was used at the end of the film.

Contemporary British fox legends seem inextricably linked to hunting and how people see foxes. Some people love foxes, urban and otherwise. Many years ago I shared a verdant garden in New Cross with the tenant of another flat, who had foxes queuing up for their nightly sausages. When she ran out of sausages she would feed them bread and jam. Others think of the fox as a ginger wolf, cunning enough to get into your house, vicious enough to attack your children and fearless enough to not be afraid when captured. The attacks on the Koupparis sisters and the story in February 2013 of a fox biting off one-month-old Denny Dolan's thumb in Bromley are shocking and terrifying, but extremely rare, considering the number of foxes in London. Whatever the individual attitudes of journalists toward foxes, a newsmaker will write and print a shocking story such as urban fox attacks, and keep the story in people's minds when foxes do less frightening things such as chewing on a pair of Ugg boots in Putney (January 2013), riding on the Circle line without a ticket (August 2012) and chewing the designer shoes of dancers in the Spiegeltent on the South Bank (September 2012). This will keep tales of fearless and ferocious foxes in the news and provide a space for people who are calling for them to be culled.

21

WHERE THE WILD THINGS ARE

✦ Big Cat Country ✦

'About 100 soldiers armed with axes and sticks joined more than 100 policemen and dogs today in a big-game hunt for a roaming leopard.' So began a story in the *London Evening News* on 17 July 1963 after a lorry driver and motorist saw a leopard in the Shooters Hill area of south-east London. 'I thought it was a dead dog,' said lorry driver David Black. 'When I got up to it, it jumped up and ran off into the wood.' When investigating this sighting the police were surprised by the beast leaping over the bonnet of their patrol car. Trackers found a clawed tree on the south-eastern side of Shooters Hill, near Welling Way, and paw prints in the mud of a dried stream. A local estate, schoolchildren and people in Woolwich Memorial Hospital, all in the area of Oxleas Wood, were warned not to go into the woods.

On 23 July, Jim Green was awoken by loud snarling noises, starting near Kidbrooke Park Road and moving along the course of the River Quaggy. A security sergeant from a nearby RAF station also heard the snarls and investigated with a police officer, seeing 'a big dark animal between 18 and 24 inches high silhouetted against a white cricket screen' at dawn.

Police said they did not know of anyone local who kept wild animals, that there was no circus in the area and no one had reported an escaped animal.

Some urban legends are straight narratives: the 'Corpse on the Tube' and the 'Accidental Theft' are stories that can be told, retold and remodelled according to their teller. Others are composed of ideas that float in the ether, waiting for an event to bring them all together again. In the case of alien big cats (ABCs) stalking Britain, and making it deep into urban London, the story first requires a witness to see an inexplicably large animal in order for the elements to come together. These folk story threads include a cat escaping from one of Britain's incontinent circuses, or a big cat that is more used to slinking about the mansion of a multi-millionaire until it escapes or is released by the bored owner. Under all this is the romantic idea that big carnivorous cats, more suited to the wild expanses of Africa and Asia, are living happily and anonymously in the suburbs and Home Counties.

Between June and August 1994 the Beast of Chiswick was seen twice a week. It was a grey or fawn colour, had a canine body and a kangaroo-like head and lived by tearing open refuse bags and disembowelling pigeons and squirrels. In June 1996 a brown big cat was spotted on a railway embankment in Northolt, prompting Doug Richardson of London Zoo to suggest to the Fortean Times that it was a mountain lion. A similar cat had been seen in Northolt in 1994. Summer 1998 saw the panther-like

'Beast of Ongar', and in 1999 an unidentified big cat was chased up a tree by a dog in Bedfords Park, Havering. In 2002 there were several sightings of a panther around the Plumstead, Bexleyheath and Shooters Hill area, including one sighting on Upton Road in Plumstead, prompting Karen Gardiner to say to the local paper *News Shopper* in October, 'I feel sorry for it not living in its natural habitat. I'd hate for it to get hurt.' By the time her husband Steve Gardiner was contacted by the *Evening Standard* on 24 January 2003, he said, 'What I remember about its size was that, as it walked away, its nose disappeared from the edge of one door while its back legs and tail were still visible in the other. Now, that's a big cat.'

The Gardiners' CCTV camera did pick up the 'panther', but after viewing the footage, Danny Bamping of the British Big Cat Society said that the film showed a 'blob', although it was a 'very large blob indeed'.

By 2005 the law of diminished returns seemed to demand that London's ABC encounters get more dramatic. Tony Holder of Sydenham was jumped by a labrador-sized cat in his garden at 2 a.m. Mr Holder had heard his pet cat making strange noises and went out to find it being held down by the beast. The ex-soldier said of the encounter: 'I could see these huge teeth and the whites of its eyes just inches from my face. It was snarling and growling and I really believed it was trying to do some serious damage. I tried to get it off but I couldn't move it, it was heavier than me.'

Perhaps because of his visible wounds (Mr Holder received a scratch on his face and arm and a wound on his finger), this was the first London big cat encounter that prompted a police response for some years. School gates were locked, people were warned not to venture in the local woods, police armed with tasers cordoned off streets and wardens warned dog walkers of the pet-bothering beast as they entered Sydenham Wells Park.

In December 2009, Roger Fleming was chased through nearby Dulwich Woods with his Staffordshire bull terrier puppy under his arm. There is no report of him contacting the police, but he did get in touch with the *News Shopper* to tell of his race against a big cat. The *News Shopper* contacted Neil Arnold of Kent Big Cat Research, who said that Mr Fleming 'should have stood his ground, maintained eye contact and backed off slowly – but it's easy to say that. People don't need to panic because big cats won't harm them.'

The response was far less drastic when a panther walked into the living room of Brian Shear, of Nunhead Lane in Zone Two Nunhead, and sat on his sofa – no one panicked at all. Diabetic Mr Shear woke up from a sleep in October 2006 having left his front door open to let in some air after feeling ill, to find that the cat had wandered into his house:

> It had green eyes and was between four to five feet long, nose to tail. This was no pussycat. It didn't miaow, it growled. I'd been sitting in my armchair when it walked in. I didn't try to get too close to it because I was concerned it might bite me. I just sat there and talked to it like you would a normal pussy cat. I said, 'Hello puss, where've you been then?' and it just growled. It seemed quite content and I didn't feel threatened. I don't think it would have harmed me. It seemed familiar with humans.

When a recent unnamed New Cross resident was 'freaked out' by seeing a panther early one morning, but the police simply asked her outright if she had been drinking, despite her sighting being in the morning and in clear daylight. She said that she had seen the cat perched over the cover of the bins of her block of flats in Southerngate Way, with its tail hanging down. Neil Arnold commented, perhaps sarcastically, 'New Cross, not far from the station – I just don't know why it would be there.'

There are plenty of witness statements regarding the big cat population of London but very little evidence of their actual existence. Dreams, hoaxes and honest misidentifications are difficult to come by, unless the hoaxer owns up to their jape or the person named in the big cat report decides that they did not actually see, were not attacked or chased by an exotic wild beast.

◇ One of our Big Cats is Missing ◇

During the 1960s and '70s in London, there were certainly some who kept big cats as 'pets'. The adventures of Christian the lion in Chelsea, bought by John Rendall and Anthony Bourke from Harrods in 1969, were documented on film and in the book *A Lion Called Christian*, published in 1971. Christian would play football in the side streets of Chelsea and was frequently taken to parties by the duo before they decided that their lion should go to Africa to live wild.

'Christian wasn't the only wild cat in this world,' Rendall told the *Guardian* in an interview published 28 May 2011. 'His neighbour was a serval cat. There was a chap in Battersea with a puma. John Aspinall had his tigers in Eaton Square and there were cheetahs and cougars roaming around Regent Street.'

The big cats of swinging London were not all fun and games, however; in January 1975 the RSPCA was called when a man left his puma in the back garden of his estranged wife and family in Acton, with a note saying he had nowhere else to keep it. The family were terrified and it took two hours to remove the animal. Another reckless puma episode took place when a man walked into the Farm House pub in South Harrow with his puma on a lead, a story that was reported in the *Daily Mirror* on 1 November 1974. Uncomfortable with feasting alongside a puma, punters asked the man to leave but the cat then ran riot in the pub, breaking glasses, destroying the bar and tables and, in proper feline fashion, the upholstery. It took fifteen minutes to get the enraged cat out of the pub and into the man's car, where the puma began to attack the upholstery. The police were called, who towed the car, cat and all, away and later charged the man with being 'drunk and incapable'.

Responding to the Acton incident, MP Peter Templemore feared that 'sooner or later someone will get killed' by a loose and barely domesticated big cat. The Dangerous Wild Animals Act became law in 1976, which made keeping a large carnivore, primate, large or venomous reptile or spider illegal without a licence. This registered the animal and allowed the local author- ity to monitor how the creature was kept. Many believe that with the coming of the Dangerous Wild Animals Act, big cat owners chose to release their pets rather than pay to register them. The legends of the urban big cats comes from the exotic pets of the 1960s and 1970s, and the new law that it is thought encouraged owners to fly-tip their problematic pumas and panthers.

Exotic animals do appear in London; a monitor lizard was believed to have been living in Geraldine Mary Harmsworth Park, next to the Imperial War Museum, for ten weeks before being rescued by the RSPCA in November 2005. In March 2003, a 'four-and-a-half-feet long and very frisky' iguana was found clinging to a tree on Wandsworth common. At first it was thought that Iggy, as RSPCA workers nicknamed the lizard, had escaped and posters were put up around the area. When no one came forward to claim him, it was thought he had been aban- doned. During December of 2011, a cold and malnourished lemur was found living on Tooting common.

The lifespan of a big cat is between twelve and fifteen years in the wild and around twenty in captivity, and probably some- where between these ages if they are living rough on squirrels and discarded takeaways. If the cats were released after 1976, as some believe, they would have died out by the mid-1990s. The urban myth of ABCs alludes to London's big cats either escaping from current homes or circuses, or being the descendants of orig- inal pumas and panthers released in the '70s. Having been made homeless, the myth suggests that the cats met in parks, around places like Plumstead or somewhere quiet in Sydenham, to mate. This would have brought about a generation of indigenous and mysterious big cats, which seems improbable. Despite the description of a big-cat infested 1960s London, it seems doubtful to me that there were enough animals to form breeding pairs. Some cryptozoologists date the cat's ancestry further back in time. In his book *Kent Urban Legends,* Neil Arnold suggests Victorian menageries provided earlier ABC stock and that London's cat community may even have its origins in Roman Britain.

One cat has been captured in the last few years, like our south London lemur and reptiles (*See* p. 171). On 4 May 2001, Carol Montague was cleaning the house of Alan and Charlotte Newman on Holcroft Avenue in Cricklewood. She looked out of the window to see a large cat, four times bigger than a domestic cat, sitting on the garden fence. Charlotte Newman then came home, saw the cat and locked her Staffordshire bull terrier in the house. At first the police laughed at the report but when two officers arrived later, they confirmed that the animal was not a domestic cat and contacted the RSPCA. The police finally took things more seriously and ten police cars arrived, including one armed response unit. Ray Charter, head zoo-keeper at London Zoo, identified the cat as a European lynx, an endangered animal, of which there were around 7,000 in 2001. After four hours a senior vet from the London Zoological Society arrived with a tranquiliser gun, just in time for the lynx to make a run for it. She was chased across playing fields and tennis courts and two hours later was cornered in the stairwell of a block of flats on Farm Avenue. She was tranquilised and taken to London Zoo to recuperate.

At the zoo she was nursed back to health, having been found very underweight and with a fracture in her left hind foot, before being sent to Zoo d'Amnéville in France to take part in the European lynx breeding programme. Happily, European lynx numbers are now at 8,000 in Europe, not counting Russia.

No licences had been obtained for lynx ownership for the area and no zoo, circus or anyone else reported a lynx missing.

Catching a misidentification of an urban big cat is a lot harder than catching an actual one. Echoing the August 2012 story of the Essex lion, on 11 March 1994 there were eight reports of a lioness prowling the area around Winchmore Hill. The first report came from a Mrs Lia Bastock, who spotted an animal with 'short golden hair and big padded paws' in Firs Lane strolling along a canal towpath. A 2.5ft-tall cat was reported slinking through local back gardens. The regular carnival arrived, namely a police helicopter along with thirty policemen combing the area and using megaphones to warn people to keep children and pets indoors. London Zoo, as ever, provided a marksman to tranquilise the beast. The cat was captured on camera sunning itself on a garden shed, and Doug Richardson of London Zoo identified the creature as a domestic cat before it was then identified as a ginger tom called Bilbo, owned by Carmel Jarvis. Carmel's cat may not have been the only one after the limelight: the *Enfield Advertiser* on 16 March 1994 revealed the cat to be Zoe Reid's pet, Twiggy.

The main story to be told about London's phantom cats is in popular mythology and sensational newspaper stories. ABCs are a nationwide phenomenon, not just a London one. Whatever the truth of the mystery of big cat sightings is, the myth is what we carry within ourselves. It is the myth we get close to whenever something strange is seen, and the answer will only come with hard evidence from the outside world.

✧ We're Going on a Bear Hunt ✧

On 27 December 1981, four boys from Lower Clapton took their dogs out for a walk across Hackney Marshes. Past Millfields Road, near the football pitches, the boys encountered 'a giant great growling hairy thing' – they met a bear in Hackney.

'We were near the football pitches at about five o'clock in the evening when we saw it,' said Darren Willoughby, aged 12. 'It was very close to us, standing on its hind legs and about seven feet tall.'

Once the press began to interview the boys, the stories began to expand. Before meeting the Hackney Bear, the boys had noticed unusual footprints in the snow, which one boy identified as bear tracks.

Following the tracks, the boys met a middle-aged couple walking their own dog and asked them if they'd seen a bear. 'Yes,' the couple replied, 'it's up there.' The couple told the boys to get away, they were near a bear after all, and to further add to the dream-like quality of events, started to throw snowballs at the boys to drive them away. This did not stop them, of course, and Tommy Murray (variously reported as 12 or 13) heard the bear growling, shone his torch on it and saw its profile standing upright in the dark. Tommy's dog, Lassie, did not want to go near it, and neither did they. The boys ran.

The police were impressed with the sincerity of the boys' fear and so launched a hunt across Hackney Marshes and along the banks of the River Lea to find the bear. Inspector Pat Curtis said, 'We do not believe this to be a hoax – we are taking no chances.'

The public were warned to keep off the marshes and not to join in with the police operation. Between fifty and 100 police officers, a police helicopter shining a searchlight over the dark ground, between fourteen and twenty dog handlers, and police marksmen armed with shotguns and handguns spent two cold days searching 8 miles of marshes and waste ground. Four RSPCA workers were concerned enough for the welfare of the bear to bring tranquiliser guns so that it could be subdued rather than assassinated, but it was clear the police were not prepared to take the risk. The Hackney Bear was 'a dangerous animal that can run faster than most men, swim and can climb trees,' Chief Inspector Platten told the press at the time. 'It will be shot dead if spotted.'

On 28 December the police searchers found footprints in the receding snow. Two sets on either side of the Lea and one on an island in the river. RSPCA inspector Derek Knight said, 'If it is a hoax it's an elaborate one. The footprints certainly look like a bear's.' Elsewhere he said, 'Perhaps not a fully grown one, maybe two or four hundredweight. But undoubtedly such a bear would be capable of killing a person.'

London Zoo director Colin Rawlings had a different view, suggesting that the bear could turn nasty 'if bothered by a dog' and that if it was a captive bear that had escaped, it would head towards people and their homes to scavenge for food rather than stay out in the wilds of Hackney. It could have hideouts, making it hard to spot.

When a shed on a local allotment had been forced open and Tommy Murray showed police the claw marks he had found on a tree, Murray told a journalist that he was 'very surprised it has not materialised'.

✧ The Bear Truth? ✧

The potential claw marks and shed-burglary were the last possible signs of the bear on the marshes and were not enough to continue the search. With disappointment looming, things began to look different. The footprints in the melting snow did not look much like bear prints. Despite a group of children telling police they had seen the bear, by the evening of 29 December police called off the search and declared Hackney Marshes safe for the public. This was not, however, the end of the story.

The next day, the *Sun* newspaper received a call from the 'Hackney bear', or at least a man named Ron who claimed to be the hoaxer behind the bear scare. Ron was inspired by an earlier bear mystery when two skinned and decapitated carcasses were found in the River Lea near Clapton on 5 December 1981, twenty-two days before the boys' sighting. A jogger had spotted two 'bodies' in the canal and at first it was thought that they were human and the victims of recent 'East End underworld' violence.

Once the bodies were identified as brown bears, a circus that had been near the river two weeks earlier was contacted but was ruled out of any enquiry. These were not the first animal bodies to appear in the Lea; others had included a puma carcass, and it was assumed that an unethical taxidermist was fly-tipping his corpses.

Their heads full of thoughts of Hackney bears, Ron and three friends dreamt up a jape whilst in the pub. They had a bear suit from a fancy dress party, so they drove out to the marshes to leave paw prints and pretend to be a bear on the loose. What Ron had not counted on was frightening the young boys enough into going to the police. 'It was only those kids who were scared,' said a nervous Ron, 'we didn't realise they would take off like that.'

The police had already looked into a fancy dress party at Flamingo Disco on Hackney Marshes on Boxing Day, the day before the first sighting. They were very interested in Ron's confession, scowling 'this has been a very expensive operation'. No doubt they were also embarrassed about the time spent shivering on the marshes whilst searching for a dangerous urban ursine entity. Being dressed up as a bear in public is not a crime as far as I know, and I am still not sure whether Ron wasted police time or whether they managed to do that themselves. There was still doubt whether Ron was telling the truth about the whole caper. A local fancy dress hire shop pointed out that bear costumes do not come with bear feet, so an outfit on its own could not leave the tracks Ron had claimed to. Perhaps he and his friends had only got as far as an idea in the pub and a telephone. Michael Goss, in his thoroughly researched article in *The Unknown*, in December 1987 to January 1988, suggests that it was the boys themselves, young and perhaps fantasy prone, who dreamt up their bear encounter.

No one else came forward to say they saw the bear and the only other evidence were suspicious scratches and paw prints.

The Ron revelation, however real, was the last thing heard about the Hackney bear for a long time. Decades later, on 17 May 2012, the *Hackney Citizen* reported a sighting of the Beast of Hackney Marshes. On the May Day bank holiday weekend, student Helen Murray was strolling through woodland near Old River Lea, a channel of the River Lea, when something large and shaggy stopped her in her tracks. She grabbed her mobile phone to dial 999 and managed to get two photographs of the creature as it moved through the undergrowth away from her. One image was of its hind quarters disappearing behind a tree, the other shows what looks like a head hunched down low from square shoulders. The two photographs show the hairy lump in the undergrowth but neither communicates movement too well.

'The "Beast of Hackney Marshes" Mystery – Pictures' trumpeted the *Hackney Gazette*, telling the story of Helen Murray's encounter, bringing newer readers up to date with the Hackney bear story and appealing for explanations. In keeping with the tradition of Ron owning up to being the Hackney bear, and two different domestic cats claiming to be the lion in Winchmore Hill, a dog owner did come forward claiming his pet was the Beast of Hackney Marshes. The dog was a Newfoundland named Willow, a huge, dark, hairy creature owned by Nicole and Paul Winter-Hart, who said they regularly walk her along Hackney Marshes. Paul was previously famous for being in the Brit Pop band Kula Shaker.

'I knew it was her immediately,' said Nicole. 'It's funny because our friends call her "The Beast" and now she's "The Beast of Hackney Marshes"!'

Helen Murray was not convinced by this explanation. While she was quick to say she thought Willow was cute, 'I'm pretty sure it wasn't a dog as it was far too big. And its build wasn't dog-like.'

The explanations for the Hackney bear are many and have become part of its myth.

22

FOLKLORE AND FAKELORE

TOWARD THE END of 2012, videos of wolves in London
appeared on YouTube. I came across one, via the Centre
for Fortean Zoology, called 'Wolves in Hackney????' It had
been uploaded on 17 November 2011 and was a convincing
piece of footage of a wolf sighted wandering up Urswick Street
in Hackney. It is apparently filmed by a couple hanging out of
an upstairs window filming fireworks when one of them looks
down and sees the wolf on the street. He shouts 'Oi!' at it while
his friend or girlfriend shushes him, but the wolf is off and runs
sleekly along the street and into the night.

Other videos appeared, including a man who had seen the remains of a dog smeared across Clapham Cfommon, and one of a couple of women singing and dancing in a living room when something big crashes over their patio. On a fourth video, a group of friends recording a birthday message to a distant friend are disturbed by a wolf in the street. They looked real; the animals intruded on films that looked natural and the creatures in the films were clearly wolves.

It was a thought that was more exciting than it was unlikely, and I shared the first wolf film I saw across Facebook and Twitter. A wise friend quickly let me know that all of the footage showing wolves marauding across London was part of a series of YouTube films to promote a brand of vodka.

This seemed like rather a convoluted way of selling alcohol. The spoof footage was seeded across the internet, people commented and then there was a reveal letting the viewer know that the films and the story attached were created to promote Eristoff Vodka. Travelling Russian show-people Davok (an anagram even I can work out) presented a 'Circus Freakout' in Victoria Park from 1–3 December 2011 with an act called 'Wolves of Vale'. A Davok van crawled through East London with banging beasts within it. Then the shows suffered a set back: 'Wolves of Vale' was cancelled due to unforeseen circumstances. Next, videos appeared on YouTube of Londoners encountering wolves or the carnage left behind by wolves. The story being told is clear: Russian wolves were loose in London. The idea presumably must have been to make the wolves a talking point and then reveal the story in a way that would encourage interested parties to toast the cleverly done spoof with a cup of the vodka they were selling. The main wolf theatre, circus vans with howls, posters and listings would only really have interested anyone in the Hackney area. The Urswick Road video, as of 18 June 2013, has had 28,741 views, about 4,106 views a month, which is better than some 'actual' cryptozoological videos such as 'Wild Black

Panther Cat Caught On Video In UK' (which averaged 962 views a month). How effective the wolves were for Eristoff sales is hard to gauge, but the vodka did drop 11 places in the May 2013 edition of 'The Power 100' list of spirits.

I emailed Us Ltd, the creative communications agency behind the campaign, to ask them what they were thinking, and whether they had been inspired by cryptozoolology in an attempt to create a buzz.

Jo Tanner of Us Ltd first responded by saying: 'Great. Love to help! Do we get paid? Royalties?'

I explained how writing local history books works to Jo and suggested the creative team would enjoy talking about their creative process. He responded: 'The idea was put together by a team of people and obviously developed as we went along.'

The thinking behind the wolves campaign was aimed at young people who are often beyond the reach of conventional advertising. '"Traditional-advertising-averse" young target audience,' as Jo put it. The wolves were there to suggest drinking Eristoff vodka to the 'young' people who are interested in 'Twilight-type stuff'. The brand values of Eristoff vodka were described as 'dark and mysterious', and their logo is a wolf. I had already suggested that out-of-place animals and vodka are not an intuitive connection, to which Jo pointed out, 'Well they are when you realise that there's a wolf in the brand's logo based on its roots being Georgian.'

✧ The Thames Angel ✧

While on her way to meet a friend along the South Bank in May 2006, Jemima Waterhouse, a 16-year-old student from Sheen, saw an angel. 'I felt a sense of calm spreading over me. It was comforting and familiar – a kind of peace that lasted for a while after. It is really hard to put into words, but I guess you could describe it as peace of mind.'

She took a photograph which appeared in the *South London Press* on 15 September 2006, who described the angel as having some sort of celebrity and gathering a fanbase:

> Eerily so far this year four people claim to have seen the angel near the London Eye and an internet cult is growing ... These sightings have prompted much online chat about the so-called Angel of the Thames. Already angel walks are being offered along the waterside and Angel T-shirts are available. One angel obsessive – who meets up with other people who have spotted the ghostly figure to share their experiences – thinks it must date back to the fire.

That's the Great Fire of London, which was apparently one of the angel's earliest recorded sightings. Three websites devoted to the Thames Angel appeared in the wake of the article. The Angel of the Thames: Have You Seen the Angel website repeated Jemima's story and wanted to collect more. The Friends of the Thames Angel blog styled itself as the official Thames Angel fan club, complete with parties and a pug dog dressed up as an angel. Thames Angel: A History of the Angel of Promise is all swirly fonts, walking guides in period costume and historical events with a Thames Angel link to them. All three sites pass on the same information in the same way: that the River Thames has a resident angel that appears in times of great strife, or to please or beguile tourists.

Photographs showing a wispy, white-winged figure amongst or behind a group of tourists are placed alongside augmented etchings of a more traditional angel to illustrate a timeline that begins in 1667. There are a lot of images, and in the photographs the angel looks almost the same in all of them.

London's history, from the Great Plague to the Blitz, is alluded to, and the angel is said to have made an appearance during the rebuilding of London after the Great Fire. The most convincing piece of 'evidence' was footage of singer and television presenter David Grant filming on the Thames being distracted by the angel. 'Did you see that?' he asks. 'Did you see it 'cos I thought it looked like ... this is ridiculous, but I think it looked like an angel.' In another piece of footage a reporter from Slovakian Television hassled David Grant to find out what he knew but, the website suggests, he has been 'got to' and did not wish to talk. There is now a conspiracy to prevent people talking about the Thames Angel.

People began to look into these websites and films, and the blog Transpontine, which takes an interest in south London matters, summarised the gaps in the angel story. The Slovakian Television logo was incorrect and the image used as a station ident was a picture of St Basil's in Moscow – the most direct piece of evidence was faked. All the websites were created in 2006 and ceased later that year, and there is no previous mention of the angel before that time. Samuel Pepys did not write about the Thames Angel. This was an etching on the Angel of Promise site of the construction of the Embankment with the angel hovering over it with a suspicious white outline around it. Transpontine found a sharper version of the image on Wikipedia, without the angel – another fake. As early as November 2006, contributors on a James Randi webpage – Randi being the nemesis of those making paranormal claims – looked into the source code of the websites and found in the biggest site, Angel of Promise, the phrase 'Global angels'. The Global Angels Foundation is a charity that aids impoverished and exploited children across the world, founded by Molly Bedingfield in 2004. Molly is the mother of pop stars Natasha and Daniel Bedingfield, and the charity finances its many good works in a number of ways, including sponsoring celebrities in strange challenges. The most chilling I have seen was one in which Bear Grylls was to row 22 miles down the Thames in a bath tub. David Grant, who supposedly saw the angel on film, was a sponsor of Global Angels and hosted their launch at Coutts Banks. All of the contemporary photographs of the angel look like a fuzzy white version of the Global Angels logo.

I have attempted to contact them to discuss the Thames Angel website and their possible connection to it, but so far they have been too busy to respond to my emails and telephone messages.

✧ The Brentford Griffin ✧

Further west along the Thames is Brentford, famed for its football club, Fuller's Brewery and the 'Brentford Triangle' novels by Robert Rankin. Brentford's other claim to fame is another mythical winged creature, the griffin. Griffins are mythical beasts of a higher order: they have the body of a lion but the head and wings of an eagle-like raptor. On the scale of London's mystery animals, the origin of its parakeets is a diversion and the panthers, pumas and bears are an absurd but romantic idea. The Brentford Griffin, however, is such a strange and ridiculous idea it is a surprise that people even consider it.

Like the Thames Angel, the Griffin has a history. In a letter to the *Fortean Times*, Issue 110, in May 1998, Martin Collins claimed to have heard stories of the griffin while at school in the 1950s. A family of griffins survived on Brentford Eyot (or Ait), after the first griffin was brought to Brentford by Nell Gwynn who had housed it in The Butts, Brentford. She had been given the griffin as a gift from Charles II. Somehow the griffin fell into the River Brent and was washed away to Brentford Eyot where it lived incognito after being presumed dead. Sir John Banks, a botanist who travelled with Captain Cook, brought another griffin to Brentford, where it was kept in a pagoda in Kew Gardens. After eventually escaping and mating with the first griffin living in the eyot, the griffin dynasty of Brentford was established until at least the 1980s. In the magazine *Magonia*, dated 19 May 1985, an article on Robert

Rankin's 'Great Mysteries of Brentford No. 23: the Gryphon' stated that:

> Reports of gryphons [sic] crop up with startling regularity throughout the pages of history. Dr Johnson records one he saw at Brentford's bull Fair: '… it was somewhat smaller than I had expected, but the proprietor assured me it was 'yet young' — it had the body of a lion cub and the neck, head and forelegs of a eagle … curiously formed wings issued from its shoulders.
>
> Johnson was in no doubt that the beast lived 'and was not the product of the gypsies' craft'. No further mention of the gryphon is made in his writings and one wonders what became of it. Possibly it was the same live specimen that my [RR] father saw at Olympia before the war. He was informed it was several hundred years old and was shown old showman's posters as proof.'

The griffin made its first contemporary appearance in March 1983. The Ealing *Guardian* 14 March 1983 had the front-page headline 'GRIFFIN AT LARGE – Mystery Flying Beast Sighted in Brentford' after one Kevin Chippendale saw the creature.

Mr Chippendale, of Brook Road South, claims to have seen the animal twice, both times in the gasworks:

> The first time was last summer when I saw something flying low across the ground in the gasworks. At first I thought it might be a plane, but it was too low and made no noise. I was intrigued to know what it was and as I walked past the Griffin pub realised it looked like the animal on the sign. I saw it again a couple of weeks later in exactly the same place.

More sightings followed. John Baroldi of the Watermans Arts Centre was quoted in the *Ealing Gazette* dated 15 March as saying that, 'A woman came from the park along the street. She was in an awful state. She had seen a huge bird and was obviously rather shaken by it.'

Robert Rankin, who was poet-in-residence at the Watermans Art Centre at the time, filled in some detail:

It has been a local myth for years. There were sightings of the ones prior to the last year. Previous ones go back to at least before the Second World War. A year ago a jogger called John Olssen reported seeing the bird as he was running by the arts centre. And a woman saw it from the top of a bus.

Miss Angela Keyhoe of Hanwell was on the top deck of the bus. She told the *Ealing Gazette* she was on a No. 65 bus near the art centre when she saw the griffin perched on top of a gasometer.

That griffins haunt Brentford may not be such a surprise: Fuller's, the local brewery, has a Griffin as a logo and they brew at the Griffin Brewery; there is a Griffin pub and Brentford Football Club's ground is Griffin Park. With the beer associations to this story it seemed fitting to meet someone who knew of the griffin in a pub but I chose one a safe distance from the Thames and Brentford, the Hermit's Cave in Camberwell.

Over pints of London-brewed ale, I learned that Robert Rankin and other locals had planned a festival in the Watermans Art Centre for 13 July 1985. This unfortunately coincided with Live Aid taking place at Wembley Stadium. To rustle up some publicity for the event, Rankin and friends, including a journalist or two, cooked up the story of a griffin being seen around the arts centre. All of the main witnesses were in on the joke; Robert Rankin wrote a historical back story for the griffin and let the idea of the creature loose. But then a strange thing happened. Brentfordians loved the idea of the griffin and took it to their hearts. The letter to the May 1998 edition of the *Fortean Times* (*See* page 83) did not, as far as my contact knew, have links with the original jape. When investigating the griffin myth for a lecture in 2003, John Rimmer, of *Magonia* magazine, went into the local pubs and the drinkers were keen to talk to him about 'their' griffin.

'Is the Brentford Griffin folklore or fakelore?' I asked my contact.

'It started out as fakelore,' he said, 'but it has become a part of Brentford folklore.'

BIBLIOGRAPHY

THIS BOOK IS made up of countless references from websites, magazine articles and newspaper stories. Where possible I have quoted the source in the text. Urban legend research is an ongoing joy and I am keen to discuss any ideas about any of the urban legends discussed in this book and others. Please contact me on skitster@hotmail.com or at the blog http://living-lore.blogspot.co.uk.

Arnold, Catharine, *Necropolis: London and Its Dead* (London: Pocket Books, 2007)

Arnold, Neil, *Kent Urban Legends: The Phantom Hitch-Hiker and Other Stories* (Stroud: The History Press, 2013)

Barber, Mark, *Urban Legends: An Investigation into the Truth Behind the Legends* (Chichester: Summersdale, 2007)

Bard, Robert, *Graveyard London: Lost and Forgotten Burial Grounds* (London: Historical Publications, 2008)

Barnett, Richard, *Sick City: Two Thousand Years of Life and Death in London* (London: Strange Attractor Press, 2008)

Bell, Karl, *The Legend of Spring-heeled Jack: Victorian Urban Folklore and Popular Cultures* (Woodbridge: Boydell Press, 2012)

Bloom, Clive, *Violent London: 2000 Years of Riots, Rebels and Revolts* (Pan Macmillan: London, 2004)

Bolton, Tom, *London's Lost Rivers: A Walker's Guide* (London: Strange Attractor Press, 2011)

Brewer, E. Cobham, *Dictionary of Phrase and Fable* (London: Cassell, 1909)

Brooks, J. A., *Ghosts of London* (Norwich: Jarrold, 1995)

Brunvand, Jan Harold, *The Choking Doberman and Other 'New' Urban Legends* (London: W.W. Norton & Co., 1986)

———, *The Mexican Pet: More 'New' Urban Legends and Some Old Favorites* (London: Penguin, 1986)

———, *Curses! Broiled Again! The Hottest Urban Legends Going* (London: W.W. Norton & Co., 1989)

———, *The Vanishing Hitchhiker: Urban Legends and their Meanings* (London: Pan Books, 1983)

Bucazacki, Stefan, *Fauna Britannica* (London: Hamlyn, 2002)

Clark, James, *Haunted London* (Stroud: Tempus Publishing, 2007)

———, *Mysterious Mitcham* (Mitcham: Shadowtime Publishing, 2002)

Clayton, Antony, *The Folklore of London* (London: Historical Publications, 2008)

Dale, Rodney, *The Tumour in the Whale* (London: Gerald Duckworth & Co., 1978)

———, *The Wordsworth Book of Urban Legends* (Hertfordshire: Wordsworth War, 2005)

———, *It's True … It Happened to a Friend* (London: Gerald Duckworth & Co., 1984)

Fort, Charles, *Lo!* (London: John Brown, 1997)

Glinert, Ed, *The London Compendium* (London: Penguin, 2004)

Halliday, Stephen, *Amazing and Extraordinary London Underground Facts* (Cincinnati: David & Charles, 2009)

Hart, Edward J., *101 London Oddities* (Sussex: J. R. Stallwood Publications, 1994)

Hayward, James, *Myths and Legends of the First World War* (Stroud: Sutton Publishing, 2002)

———, *Myths and Legends of the Second World War* (Stroud: Sutton Publishing, 2003)

Ibrahim, Mecca, *One Stop Short of Barking: Uncovering the London Underground* (London: New Holland, 2004)

Jackson, Peter, *London Explorer* (London: Associated Newspapers, 1953)

————, *London is Stranger than Fiction* (London: Associated Newspaper, 1951)

Jacobson, David J., *The Affairs of Dame Rumour* (New York: Rinehart, 1948)

Jenkins, Alan C., *Wildlife in the City* (Exeter: Webb & Bower, 1982)

Jones, Christopher, *Subterranean Southwark* (London: Past Tense, 2003)

Kempe, David, *Living Underground* (London: Herbert Press, 1988)

Kent, William, *The Lost Treasures of London* (London: Phoenix House, 1947)

————, *Walks in London* (London: Staples Press, 1951)

Long, Roger, *Historic Inns along the River Thames* (Stroud: Sutton Publishing, 2006)

Pyeatt, Samuel Menefee, 'Megalithic Movement: A Study of Thresholds in Time' in Davidson, Hilda Ellis (ed.), *Boundaries & Thresholds: Papers from a Colloquium of The Katharine Briggs Club* (Stroud: The Thimble Press, 1993)

Roberts, Chris, *Football Voodoo: Magic, Superstition and Religion in the Beautiful Game* (London: F&M Publications, 2010)

Rogers, Cyril H., *Parrots* (London: W&G Foyle, 1958)

Roud, Steve, *London Lore* (London: Random House, 2008)

Screeton, Paul, *Mars Bars & Mushy Peas: Urban Legends and the Cult of Celebrity* (Loughborough: Heart of Albion, 2008)

Smith, Paul, *The Book of Nasty Legends* (London: Routledge & Kegan, 1983)

————, *The Book of Nastier Legends* (London: Routledge & Kegan, 1986)

Smith, Stephen, *Underground London: Travels Beneath the City Streets* (London: Abacus, 2007)

Swinnerton, Jo (ed.), *The London Companion* (London: Robson, 2004)

Thornbury, Walter, *Old and New London Volume II* (London: Cassell Petter & Galpin, 1878)

Walford, Edward, *London Recollected: Its History, Lore and Legend* (London: Alderman, 1985)

White, Jerry, *Rothschild Buildings: Life in an East End Tenement Block 1887–1920* (London: Pimlico, 2003)

Willey, Russ, *Brewer's Dictionary of London Phrase & Fable* (London: Chambers, 2009)

❖ A Selection of Magazines and Websites ❖

Fortean Times – www.forteantimes.com

FLS News (Folklore Society) – www.folklore-society.com

Magonia – www.magonia.haaan.com

The Unknown

Urban Legend Resource (Snopes) – www.snopes.com

Alexander McQueen obituary: www.news.bbc.co.uk

Design Museum: www.designmuseum.org

'Dressed To Thrill': www.newyorker.com

'Porno magazines found in Queen's Car': www.thefreelibrary.com

'Secrets and lies: Shroud Origins of Giant Swastika': www.msgboard.snopes.com

'We Are Not Amused: Jag Man's Swastika Prank Backfires': www.thefreelibrary.com

Argyll Arms: www.nicholsonspubs.co.uk

King and Tinker pub: www.kingandtinker.co.uk/

Michael Jackson at the Montague Arms: www.transpont.blogspot.co.uk

The Old Watling: www.nicholsonspubs.co.uk/

Travel UK: 'Where Rivals Feared to Tread': www.independent.co.uk

Wimbledon tunnel: www.thisislocallondon.co.uk

'Suicidal Architects' p.7 FLS News, No.37, June 2002

'Suicidal Sculptor' p.13 FLS News, No.57, February 2009

Eagle Pillar: www.geograph.org.uk
The Chain Bridge Lions: www.bridgesofbudapest.com
The Seriousness of Mormon Humour:
   www.thejazzy.tripod.com
The Devils of Cornhill: www.shadyoldlady.com

If you enjoyed this book, you may also be interested in …

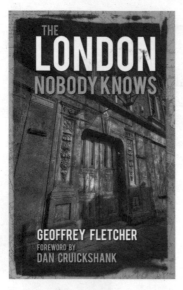

The London Nobody Knows
Geoffrey Fletcher

Geoffrey Fletcher's off-beat portrayal of London does not focus on the big landmarks, but rather 'tawdry, extravagant and eccentric'. His descriptio will transport you to an art nouveau pub, a Victo music hall, a Hawksmoor church and even a public toilet in Holborn in which the attendant kept goldfish in the cisterns. Drawn to the corne where 'the kids swarm like ants and there are do everywhere', Fletcher will take you to parts of th where few outsiders venture. Originally publishe 1962, in 1967 *The London Nobody Knows* was tur into an acclaimed documentary film starring Jam Mason. This book has been a must-have for anyo with an interest in London ever since.

978 0 7524 6199 1

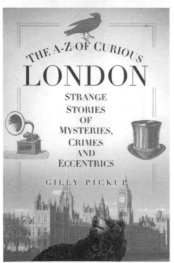

The A-Z of Curious London: Strange Stories of Mysteries Crimes and Eccentrics
Gilly Pickup

Spooky, gruesome, weird but true things about o of the world's greatest cities come alive in *The A of Curious London*. Discover London's tiniest hou 4,000-year-old mouse made from Nile clay, and a giggle at things people leave on London's trans Why did a dentist keep his dead wife on view in shop window? Which Queen showed her boson an Ambassador? Why was a man arrested for we a top hat? To sum up, eccentrics, legends, folklor murders, scandals, ghosts, incredible characters ar oodles of wow factor – it's all here.

978 0 7524 8968 1

Visit our website and discover thousands of other History Press books.

www.thehistorypress.co.uk

The Histc Pres